BREAKING the CHAINS

The Crusade
of
Dorothea Lynde Dix

Other Books by Penny Colman:

Dark Closets and Noises in the Night
I Never Do Anything Bad
Grand Canyon Magic
Betsy Ross: Sharp Eyes and Nimble Fingers
Fifty Years Together, co-author with Stella Chess, M.D. and
    Alexander Thomas, M.D.

BREAKING the CHAINS

The Crusade
of
Dorothea Lynde Dix

Penny Colman

SHOE TREE PRESS
WHITE HALL, VIRGINIA

Published by Shoe Tree Press, an imprint of
Betterway Publications, Inc.
P.O. Box 219
Crozet, VA 22932
(804) 823-5661

Cover design by Rick Britton
Cover photograph by permission of Houghton Library,
Harvard University. Dorothea Dix at age eighteen.
Typography by Park Lane Associates

Library of Congress Cataloging-in-Publication Data

Colman, Penny
    Breaking the chains : the crusade of Dorothea Lynde Dix /
Penny Colman.
       p. cm.
    Includes bibliographical references and index.
    Summary: Recounts Dorothea Dix's lifelong fight to improve
the lives of others, such as her own family, the mentally ill,
prisoners, the physically ill, and the retarded.
    ISBN 1-55870-219-9 (pbk.) : $5.95
    1. Dix, Dorothea Lynde, 1802-1887--Juvenile literature. 2.
Social reformers--United States--Biography--Juvenile literature. [1.
Dix, Dorothea Lynde, 1802-1887. 2. Reformers.] I. Title.
    HV28.D6C65 1991
    361.92--dc20
  [B]   91-17986
                                       CIP
                                       AC

Printed in the United States of America
0 9 8 7 6 5 4 3 2 1

For Jonathan, David, and Stephen, with love.

ACKNOWLEDGMENTS

Special thanks to Linda Hickson Bilsky for sharing my enthusiasm and for reading this manuscript over and over again.

Special thanks also go to the following librarians and archivists: Joan Leopold, Dorothea Dix Library and Museum, Harrisburg, Pennsylvania; Katherine W. Trickey, Hampden Historical Society, Hampden, Maine; Kristi C. Heesch, Unitarian Universalist Association, Boston, Massachusetts; David J. Johnson, The Casement Museum, Fort Monroe, Virginia; Jan Lazarus, National Library of Medicine, Washington, DC; Ann Sparanese, Englewood Public Library, Englewood, New Jersey; and Greg Imbroglia, Elaine Scheuerer, and Frank Cuano, Trenton Psychatric Hospital, Trenton, New Jersey.

CONTENTS

Chapter One

HARD TIMES: 1802-1809

Dorothea Lynde Dix was a difficult woman—strong-willed, determined, opinionated, and outspoken. Nevertheless, when she died in 1887, people around the world honored her. Proclamations, testimonials, and tributes were spoken and printed from the United States to Japan to England. A prominent American doctor wrote, "Thus had died and been laid to rest in the most quiet, unostentatious way the most useful and distinguished woman America has yet produced." Almost a hundred years after her death, the United States Postal Service selected Dorothea Dix to be pictured on a one-cent stamp. Few American women have been honored in this way.

Today most people don't know who Dorothea Dix was or why her face is on a postage stamp. That would please her. She always shunned publicity for herself. She refused to let anything be written about her. Once, when a person asked for permission to write about her career, Dorothea Dix replied, "I feel it right to say to you frankly that nothing could be undertaken which would give me more pain and serious annoyance, which would so trespass on my personal right ... or interfere more seriously with the real usefulness of my mission."

11

Nor would she agree to write anything herself, "There is, I think, great difficulty in writing of one's self: it is almost impossible to present subjects where the chief actor must be conspicuous, and not seem to be, or really be egotistical."

But Dorothea Dix's life is too important to forget. Like many people, she wanted her life to matter — to mean something. She wanted to make the world a better place. And, despite great difficulties, Dorothea Lynde Dix did.

Dorothea Lynde Dix (she was christened Dorothy after her grandmother) was born on April 4, 1802 in Hampden, Maine. Today the land where Dorothea Dix's house stood is called the Dorothea Dix Park. A huge stone arch stands as a memorial to Dorothea Dix with a plaque that reads:

In Memory of
Dorothea Lynde Dix
who by devoted care to sick and wounded sol-
diers during the Civil War earned the gratitude of
the Nation, and by her labors in the cause of
prison reform and of humane treatment of the in-
sane won the admiration and reverence of the
civilized world.
1802-1887
Her Birthplace.

When Dorothea Dix was born, Thomas Jefferson was President of the United States, and there were only sixteen states. Maine wasn't one of them yet; it was still part of the state of Massachusetts. Hampden was built out of the wilderness above the banks of the Penobscot River. The first settler, Benjamin Wheeler, had traveled up the Penobscot River in the summer of 1767. Near where the Sowadabscook Stream flows into the Penob-

Front of an envelope issued on September 23, 1983, in celebration of the postage stamp honoring Dorothea Dix.

scot, Wheeler discovered swiftly flowing, clear, cold water and lots of game and fish. After a dinner of roast partridge, Wheeler spent the night on the shore, then headed home the next morning to get his family and return.

Soon Wheeler's spot attracted other people and the town of Wheelersborough was incorporated in 1774. It was renamed Hampden in 1795 after an English patriot, John Hampden, who died while fighting with the Americans during the Revolutionary War.

Elihu Hewes, who arrived in 1775, described the area in this way: "I find this country very good for both tillage and grass though at present clothed with a fine growth of pine, cedar, hemlock, and interspersed with large spots of rock and white maple, birch, beach, etc. and some oak. The river excels for fish of various kinds and easy navigation for the largest vessels."

By 1802 about 200 families lived in wood houses on 100-acre lots (anything smaller than 100 acres wasn't big enough to support a family). Cash was scarce and people either grew or made what they needed, or they bartered for what they couldn't produce themselves. To get in and out of Hampden, travelers went by boat. A trip through the woods by wagon, or by sleigh in the winter, was an extremely slow, bone-rattling experience. According to town records, the biggest problem in Hampden in the early 1800s was the number of pigs and sheep running around loose. After much discussion, the Selectmen, or town officials, finally decided to build an animal pound out of peeled white pine logs. Gooden Grant was appointed the pound keeper. In addition to the pound, Hampden had 111 dwellings, 5 shops, 1 tannery, 1 potash factory, 8 warehouses, 2 grist mills, 1 saw mill, 72 barns, 62 horses, 115 oxen, 274 cows, and 182 swine. There was also a jail, a courthouse, a church, a school house, a post office, and two shipyards—one at the end of Elm Street east and the other at Higgins Yard.

Ships were also built at Pitcher's Brook and East Hampden. These were big ships—schooners between 100-125 tons and full-sized ships that sailed to the West Indies loaded with lumber and flour and returned with molasses, sugar, and rum. By the time of Dorothea Dix's birth, Hampden bustled with the sights, sounds, and smells of a thriving port.

Dorothea Dix's parents, Joseph Dix and Mary Bigelow Dix, hadn't chosen to live in Hampden. Rather they were sent there by Joseph's father, Elijah Dix, a successful Boston doctor and businessman who had purchased vast acres of land in Maine as an investment. Joseph had met Mary Bigelow, who was eighteen years older than he, when he was studying for the ministry at Harvard. Undoubtedly his parents were troubled by the age difference, but even worse than that, they considered Mary Bigelow uncouth, ignorant, and ill-fitted to marry a Dix. However, their disapproval—and the fact that as a married man he would have to leave Harvard—didn't stop Joseph from marrying Mary. Supporting himself and his wife wasn't quite so easy. Finally Joseph agreed to go to Maine and manage his father's land, which included two towns Elijah Dix had founded—Dixmont, twenty miles from Hampden, and Dixfield, another 100 miles away. Living in Maine and managing the land required enormous fortitude: the winters were long and cold, and spring was knee-deep in mud. Roads and bridges were nonexistent; travel was limited to waterways or along blazed trails through dense forests. Under these conditions, Joseph Dix was supposed to convince people to settle in Maine.

In addition, like everybody else in Hampden who wanted to eat, Joseph was also supposed to farm the 100 acres around their house. He wasn't good at either task; neither selling real estate nor farming interested him. His only interest, which soon became an obsession, was preaching about heaven and hell. Saving souls was more important than filling stomachs. Joseph Dix's conviction was so strong that he was determined, as he said, "to carry the gospel to the farthest settlements."

For days and weeks at a time, Joseph rode his horse afar and sermonized about sin and salvation. Dorothea and her mother managed alone. When Dorothea was four years old, her brother Joseph was born. Her mother, never emotionally or physically strong, spent more and more time in bed, and Dorothea took on more and more responsibility. She washed dishes in the wooden sink, cleaned the house with its bare floors made from split logs and windows with panes of oiled paper, cooked whatever meager amounts of food they had, and cared for Joseph and her mother.

Frontier life was hard. The tasks were endless: knitting socks, piecing quilts, making butter and cheese,

15

mending clothes, clearing fields, making soap and candles, drying vegetables, curing meat, spinning and weaving and dyeing cloth, and gathering herbs, nuts, and wild fruit. If the family was to survive, Dorothea had to grow up very fast.

Worst of all, Dorothea had to make books out of the pages of sermons her father wrote. Hour after hour she pushed and pulled a big needle threaded with heavy thread through a thick stack of papers. Despite cracked and calloused fingers, Dorothea persevered because the books were the only thing her father could sell or barter for food.

Dorothea Dix's grandparents, Elijah and Dorothy Lynde Dix, offered the only relief in her dismal life. They lived in Dix Mansion, a great red brick house topped with a cupola, on Orange Court in Boston. It had plate glass windows, high scrolled ceilings, carved wainscotings, beautiful furniture, pictures on the walls, fine carpets, and beautiful flower gardens. Dorothea's father, Joseph, the third of Elijah's and Dorothy's seven sons and one daughter, had grown up there. Dorothea's only happiness came when she visited her grandparents at Dix Mansion.

Her grandmother was a woman of refined manners, strict discipline, and generous hospitality. Her grandfather was ambitious and shrewd, with a quick wit and an even quicker temper. A man of enormous energy and a variety of interests, Elijah Dix had a special affection for Dorothea. He filled her head with stories about his growing up, about the Revolutionary War, and about his travels. One of Dorothea's favorite stories was about how he outwitted a group of men he had offended with his quick temper. According to Dr. Dix, he found out that the men planned to get revenge and physically harm him. So Dr. Dix was ready when a man showed up one night and asked him to visit a sick patient a few miles out of town. The doctor agreed to go, but first instructed his servant to: "Bring round my horse at once; see that the pistols in my holsters are double-shotted; then give the bulldog a piece of raw meat and turn him loose to go along!" At which point, Dr. Dix would end the story with a dramatic flourish that Dorothea loved, "the man quietly disappeared into the night."

Whenever Dorothea came to Boston, her grandfather delighted in taking her with him when he visited patients or went to his apothecary shop, where she marvelled at the bottles of leeches, minerals, and pills. He showed her the pear tree he had developed by grafting and crossing one tree with another to produce the best-tasting pears in the country. Together they examined items from the West Indies and China — brought to Boston on ships Dr. Dix owned.

Periodically Dr. Dix came to Hampden to check on his land business and the conditions in Dixmont and Dixfield. After spending time with Dorothea, he'd go off on horseback, traveling throughout the area, always ready to sell a settler more land. During one of these excursions Elijah Dix collapsed and died. According to a local legend still alive today, Dr. Dix collapsed just before signing a deed. Quickly the buyer, seeing a golden opportunity, put a fly in Dr. Dix's mouth. "There's still life in there," the buyer said, motioning for witnesses to come closer and listen to the fly buzzing. Then the buyer grasped Dr. Dix's hand in his hand, stuck a pen between the limp fingers, and signed the deed.

Elijah Dix was buried in a cemetery on the side of a hill in Dixmont. These words were carved on his gravestone:

In Memory of Doctor Elijah Dix
of Boston
who deceased in this town
(of which he was the founder)
May 28, 1809
Aged 62
A man distinguished by strength of mind
active industry
and arduous enterprise.

Dorothea was seven years old when her beloved grandfather died. Fortunately, his characteristics engraved on his gravestone—strength of mind, arduous enterprise, and active industry—didn't die with him; from an early age, they were apparent in Dorothea Lynde Dix. And she needed them as the burdens of her life weighed heavier. Another brother, Charles Wesley, had been born, her father became more fanatical about his religion, and her mother became more of an emotional and physical invalid.

As an adult Dorothea Dix refused to talk about her early years. "I never knew a childhood!" is all she would say.

Chapter Two

GROWING UP FAST: 1802-1821

Nothing is known about Dorothea Dix's early education. But it's reasonable to assume that her well-educated father taught her how to read and write, since children were required to know these skills before they could start school. Given the Dix's financial situation, Dorothea probably attended the public grammar school in Hampden instead of the private academy that had been founded the year she was born.

Located not far from Dorothea Dix's home, the grammar school was originally built with two windows on each side for light. However, by the time Dorothea Dix took her place on the plank seat, the windows had been closed on one side and added to the rear because some experts had convinced people that light coming from both sides, or cross light, was harmful to children. As was the custom, Dorothea Dix would have attended school with the girls during the summer term from April through September when the boys went to work in the fields.

Although Joseph Dix's fame as a preacher spread —he was noted for the depth of his conviction and his engaging personality — he continued to fail as a provider. It is not known how long the family stayed in

Hampden, although Dorothea Dix once remarked during the Civil War that she had not seen Hampden since she was ten years old. Whenever they left, it's clear they made at least several moves, including one to Bernard, Vermont where Joseph Dix opened a shop and sold, according to an old handbill, "a handsome and useful assortment of miscellaneous books, also schoolbooks, singly or by the dozen, at Boston prices. Cash or produce taken in payment."

When she was twelve years old, Dorothea Dix's life changed dramatically. Whether she ran away or was sent by her parents or was asked for by her grandmother is unknown; what is known is that Dorothea Dix ended up living with Madam Dix at Dix Mansion—where she was finally free from the relentless instability, unhappiness, and hardship of her own home.

Unfortunately, life with Madam Dix proved to have a different set of difficulties. Sixty-eight years old when Dorothea arrived to stay, Madam Dix was determined to teach her granddaughter the proper values of a white, upper middle class urban woman — neatness, punctuality, obedience, subservience to men, and meticulousness in everything she did; values of little relevance to the frontier existence Dorothea Dix had survived before moving to Dix Mansion.

The eighth child of Joseph and Mary Lynde's seventeen children, Madam Dix grew up in Worcester, Massachusetts and received the best possible education and training. Known as the "belle of Worcester" when she was a young woman, Madam Dix was determined that Dorothea become a proper woman according to nineteenth century standards.

The nineteenth century, or 1800s, was a time of astonishing economic and social change in America. Towns and cities were filling up with people. Factories were being built. Women could buy velvet made in a factory in Newark, New Jersey and silk made in Paterson, New Jersey, instead of weaving and dyeing fabric themselves. Or they could buy wallpaper made in New Brunswick instead of whitewashing or stenciling their walls by hand. Increasingly boys grew up to become men who spent their days earning a living doing business in an office. Girls grew up to become wives who stayed at home to manage the household and "to constantly endeavor to render him [their husband] more virtuous, more useful, more honourable, and more happy," in the words of the Reverend Samuel Miller.

According to nineteenth century advice books, an ideal woman needed to learn four things — religious piety, sexual purity, wifely submission, and motherly domesticity. And adolescence was the prime time to acquire these attributes. It was the time, according to a prominent nineteenth century physician, when girls shed the "light and airy habiliments of girlhood" and put on "the more staid and dignified mantle of womanhood."

Dorothea Dix wanted no part of it. But Madam Dix persisted. Over and over again Madam Dix made Dorothea tear out stitches in her embroidery until they were perfect. She insisted Dorothea bundle up her energy and learn how to walk and dance properly. And she tried repeatedly to channel Dorothea's intellectual curiosity into such domestic tasks as managing servants and entertaining elegantly.

Time and time again, Dorothea Dix and her grandmother, who were both strong-willed women, clashed. It wasn't easy for Dorothea to give into Madam Dix, especially after assuming so many burdens and responsibilities for her parents and brothers. Finally Dorothea was sent to Worcester to live with Madam Dix's sister, Sarah Lynde Duncan, and her husband, William Duncan.

Dorothea Dix's stay in Worcester lasted only a few

years, but they were happy years. Great-aunt Sarah, her married daughter Sarah Lynde Fiske, and a host of cousins, great-aunts, and uncles welcomed Dorothea into their swirl of family activities. Infinitely more tactful and understanding than her sister in Dix Mansion, Great-aunt Sarah guided Dorothea until she was, in the words of one Worcester relative, "very much improved in manners and habits of neatness."

When she was barely fourteen years old, Dorothea Dix announced that she wanted to start a school in Worcester for young children. It would be what was called a "dame" or "marm" school, in which she would teach basic reading and writing skills to three- and four-year-old children.

Great-aunt Sarah and Sarah Fiske agreed because teaching school was a logical choice for Dorothea. Teaching was considered a proper profession for genteel white New England women, and Dorothea was noted for her quick mind and passion for learning. With the two Sarahs' help, Dorothea Dix enlisted pupils, many from the best families in Worcester, including the sons of a future governor of Massachusetts and two students who themselves grew up to be famous teachers, Anne Bancroft and Lucy Green.

Dorothea Dix's school opened in an empty classroom in the public schoolhouse near the corner of Main and Central. Soon the enrollment increased to as many as twenty children at one time, so Dix moved her school to a vacant store building. She loved teaching. "The duties of a teacher are neither few nor easy," Dorothea Dix once wrote to a friend, "but they elevate the mind and give energy to the character."

To compensate for her youth, Dorothea Dix wore the fashions and hair style of a grown woman and was described at the time as being "tall, erect, slight, good looking; neither very light nor very dark; with a round face and a very stern decided expression." Another student described her "as easily blushing, at once beautiful and imposing in manner, but inexorably strict in discipline."

According to all accounts, Dorothea Dix was a strict, tough disciplinarian. In the context of the times, however, her tactics were considered appropriate, necessary, and wise—"spare the rod and spoil the child" was considered the gospel truth. William Lincoln, one of the sons of the future governor, didn't pass a day in Dorothea Dix's school without feeling her birch-rod. In a discussion years later, Lincoln, who grew up to become a famous general, said, "No, I don't know that she had any special grudge against me but it was her nature to use the whip and use it, she did." Dorothea Dix was also especially harsh with her brother Joseph, who was now living with relatives in Worcester and attending his sister's school. Girls were generally spared physical punishment; their penalties lay in the power of humiliation. Years later one former female student recalled being forced to go through the streets for a week wearing a placard on her back that read, "A very bad girl, indeed."

With her characteristic forcefulness — what some contemporaries described as stubbornness—Dorothea Dix drilled her pupils in reading, writing, manners, customs, sewing, morals, and religion. Every week each child had to memorize a chapter from the Bible. On Mondays, Dix ordered the students to march to the front of the room where one by one, standing on their toes with their arms folded and faces turned upward, they recited what they had memorized for the week.

In 1819, at the age of seventeen, Dorothea Dix returned to Dix Mansion eager to continue her education. But, according to stories passed on through generations of Dorothea Dix's Worcester relatives, she left part of her heart in Worcester. Edward Dillingham Bangs, the object of her affection, was fourteen years her senior, her second cousin, and likewise attracted to Dorothea Dix. For now, however, since Boston offered more educational opportunities than Worcester, they agreed to exchange letters and visits.

Fortified by the successes of her school and warm, happy experiences with her Worcester relatives, Dorothea Dix returned to Boston confident and mature. Madam Dix welcomed her back and spared no expense in providing private instruction for Dorothea Dix in a wide range of subjects—history, literature, astronomy, botany, and languages. In addition, Dix attended public lecture courses given by Harvard professors as a way to supplement their meager incomes. She also taught herself by spending hours reading books from her grandfather's extensive library and her Uncle Thaddeus Mason Harris's library in Dorchester. Or she explored the Boston Library, the Shakespeare Library, and the American Academy with its thousands of books about science.

With her characteristic strict self-discipline and relentless determination, Dorothea Dix studied and studied. She was particularly fond of natural science, history, art, and literature. Suddenly, in 1821, two days before her birthday, Dorothea Dix's father died. Dix took stock: her brothers Joseph and Charles Wesley, already living in Dix Mansion, weren't ready to be independent; her mother would never be independent; and a fair portion of her grandmother's fortune had gone to finance the adventures of her sons, in particular William, Clarendon, and Alexander. Clearly it was time, Dorothea Lynde Dix decided, for her to earn money by opening a school. The problem was, she decided to open it in Dix Mansion. That idea appalled Madam Dix.

Chapter Three

IMPORTANT FRIENDSHIPS: 1821-1831

There was no need to have hoards of children trampling through Dix Mansion, Madam Dix said. There was enough money to last. Besides, Dorothea had to be careful of her health; it was a well-known fact that she had a tendency to have serious throat and lung problems.

She would control the children, Dorothea Dix responded. In addition, it was her responsibility to provide for her mother and brothers. As for her health, she felt fine. Back and forth they went until finally Madam Dix gave in.

Dorothea Dix started small by first opening a day school in the little house that stood near the main house. Quickly her reputation as a thorough and effective teacher spread and soon she was operating a combination boarding and day school in Dix Mansion. Children came from as far away as Portsmouth, New Hampshire to live and study at Dorothea Dix's school.

Not content to stop with her success, Dorothea Dix decided to open a second school in a room over the stables. This one would be free for poor and neglected children. Anticipating her grandmother's negative reaction to her idea, Dorothea Dix tried a new strategy. She presented her idea through a letter:

My Dear Grandmother — Had I the saint-like eloquence of our minister, I would employ it in explaining all the motives, and dwelling on all the good, good to the poor, the miserable, the idle, and the ignorant, which would follow your giving me permission to use the barn chamber for a schoolroom for charitable and religious purposes ... when it can be done without exposure or expense, let me rescue some of America's miserable children from vice and guilt? ... Do, my dear grandmother yield to my request, and witness next summer the reward of your benevolence and Christian compliance.

Your affectionate Granddaughter D.L. Dix

Reluctantly Madam Dix agreed — once again Dorothea Dix's ability to persuade people worked.

Dorothea Dix labored long and hard. Up at four a.m. in the summer and five a.m. in the winter, she always worked past midnight teaching, studying, and writing. "You know well," she wrote to a friend, "that the measure of my days is filled with constant business, teaching, and learning, reading, and writing, sewing, and mark[et]ing seem to leave me little leisure for amusement of any kind!" In addition, she kept a close eye on her brothers and cared for Madam Dix, whose health was failing. But it was worth it. For, as Dorothea Dix wrote to a friend, "To me, the avocation of a teacher has something elevating and exciting. While surrounded by the young, one may always be doing good."

Dorothea Dix loved being in Boston. A city of about 40,000 people, Boston was bustling with new ideas and activities. The harbor was white with sails of great ships, schooners, and sloops laden with cargo from faraway lands. Great thinkers such as Senator Daniel Webster and the Reverend Ralph Waldo Emerson walked along footpaths lined with towering trees—oak, sycamore, maple, linden—in the huge open park called the Commons beside the newly completed capitol building with its shiny golden dome. Merchants, shoppers, university students, and craftspeople crowded the narrow dirt or cobbled streets. And there were traders who herded livestock along the streets to the docks while they watched out for pranksters who loved to grab a pig and throw it in a store or at an innocent passerby. Originally paths made by cows when the land was a pasture, the streets twisted and turned past three- and four-story brick and granite houses with steep gables, dormers, and tall skinny chimneys that looked like a forest in the sky.

Intermingled with the chimneys were the white steeples of the seventy churches located throughout Boston. Every Sunday Dorothea Dix sat with her grandmother in the Dix family pew at the Congregational Church on Hollis Street; that is, until she met the minister at the Unitarian Church on Federal Street, Dr. William Ellery Channing. A small, shy man, Channing was an inspiring preacher and teacher. The leader of the Unitarians, a new religious group that had recently broken away from the Congregational Church, Channing preached that "the supreme good of an intelligent and moral being is the perfection of its nature."

Dorothea Dix was drawn to his belief in the essential goodness of people. It was such a relief after the constant specter of eternal damnation in her father's preachings. Despite Madam Dix's disapproval, Dorothea Dix attended Channing's church and developed a close friendship with him and his family.

The demands of her life left Dorothea Dix little time for leisure, not that she minded. "I have little taste for fashionable dissipations, cards, & dancing;" she wrote to a friend, "the theatre and tea parties are my

*William Ellery Channing,
Dorothea Dix's mentor.
(Photo courtesy of Unitarian
Universalist Association.)*

aversion, and I look with little envy on those who find their enjoyment in such transitory delights, if delights they must be called." Occasionally she made an exception, as when the Marquis de Lafayette, the French hero who fought for the Americans in the Revolutionary War, came to Boston. "This evening I am to be presented to the Marquis & dare not think what I shall appear like but fear like a simpleton. I half dread going but I may never enjoy the opportunity again so shall summon all my courage and confidence to meet the emergency of the case."

Tall, slight but well proportioned, attractive with a bright, intelligent expression, and with an abundance of red-brown hair, Dorothea Dix always dressed simply. Her directness and intelligence drew people to her and, according to one person who observed her at a reception, Dorothea Dix always "looked sweet and was very much admired." Later in life, after she became famous, there were many reports of Dorothea Dix's striking beauty, compelling personality, and unique

A letter from Millard Fillmore when he was President of the United States to Dorothea Dix in which he writes, "Please to accept the accompanying bouquet as a slight testimony of the respect and esteem, with which your disinterested devotion to the cause of suffering humanity, has inspired you. Sincere friend, Millard Fillmore." Dix and Fillmore had a long-term and close friendship. (Reproduced by permission of the Houghton Library, Harvard University.)

ability to have intellectual discussions with men despite their belief that women were supposed to be seen, not heard.

Although Dorothea Dix disliked social gatherings, she loved visiting people and developing personal friendships. Throughout her lifetime she had a wide circle of devoted friends, including many of the most prominent people of the nineteenth century. In the days before the telephone was invented, Dorothea Dix was a dedicated letter writer, as were most educated people. Back and forth letters went between her and poets like John Greenleaf Whittier, novelists like Fredrika Bremer, politicians like President Millard Fillmore, physicians like Luther V. Bell, and educators like Horace Mann.

Of all her correspondence, the longest and most intense was with her closest friend and confidante, Anne Eliza Heath. For fifty-five years the two women exchanged their deepest thoughts, secret ambitions, successes, bits of gossip, concern for each other's health, frustrations, and sorrows. "Dear Annie," Dorothea Dix would start her letters and frequently close with "Thea." "Dear Theodora," Anne Heath would write back.

During the early years of their friendship, they wrote two, three, even four times a week despite being teased by their friends and family. Each letter was carefully written on three sides of double sheets of pale blue or white note paper, carefully folded and addressed. Then, instead of sealing their letters with a glob of hot wax like most people did, "Dear Annie" and "Thea" stitched the edges together with a needle and thread.

Three years older than Dorothea Dix, Anne Heath lived near Boston in a large white house in Brookline, Massachusetts, at the top of a hill overlooking a valley.

She was part of a large and happy family that Dorothea Dix loved to visit. "I always leave your house with regret," Dix told her in a letter, "and feel that there I might always be happy."

Their correspondence began in 1823 when Dorothea Dix was twenty-one years old and ended when Anne Heath died in 1878. "It was in winter that we first met," Dorothea Dix confided in a letter, "I shall ever love the chilly old season the better for that." Although Dorothea Dix instructed Anne to destroy her letters, Anne Heath kept all of them. And when "Dear Annie" died, the letters were discovered in a small chest, along with bits of pressed leaves and flowers and sprigs of evergreen that Dorothea Dix had frequently enclosed in her letters and wisps of Dorothea's hair that were carefully tied and labeled.

In her letters to Anne Heath, Dorothea Dix revealed an emotional side that she kept carefully hidden from public view. The stern, demanding teacher, the strict sister, the proper granddaughter allowed her friend to know her vulnerabilities and longings. In one early letter, Dorothea Dix wrote a poem dedicated to Anne Heath:

In the sad hour of anguish and distress
To thee for sympathy will I repair
Thy soothings sure will make my sorrows less
And what thou canst not soothe, thou will share.
Though many are to me both good and kind
And grateful still my heart shall ever be
Yet thou are to me a more congenial mind
More than a sister's love binds thee to me.

Intensely expressive friendships like the one between Dorothea Dix and Anne Heath were common among women during the nineteenth century. Trained

A letter Dorothea Dix wrote to Anne Heath after the Civil War. Written in Dix's familiar bold but difficult to decipher handwriting, the letter begins, "My dear Annie —I hope you are well." (Reproduced by permission of the Houghton Library, Harvard University.)

to be submissive, docile, and gentle in order to become proper, dutiful wives and mothers, the ideal woman learned not to express emotions or strong opinions. Whether or not a woman married, she was still expected to know her proper place. Only in the privacy of their diaries or in letters did ideal women dare express themselves freely in language that was often poetic, passionate, and intense. "Do not show or read anyone this note," Dorothea Dix frequently admonished Anne Heath at the end of particularly emotional letters.

Letters weren't the only thing Dorothea Dix wrote. In 1824 she published *Conversation on Common Things*, an enormously popular textbook for children with information about nearly 300 topics, including astronomy, nature, history, art, and literature. The book eventually appeared in sixty editions and provided Dorothea with a source of income throughout her life.

Unfortunately, the strain of writing the book in addition to all her other activities was too much. Dorothea Dix's shoulders drooped lower and lower and her voice became husky and weak. She couldn't stand in front of her students without holding onto her desk with one hand, while pressing the other hand against her side as if holding back pain. Finally, her lungs became congested, and before long Dorothea Dix was hemorrhaging and spitting up blood. By the end of 1824, she had to give up teaching. "Dear Annie—Dr. Hayward thinks I must be very careful," she wrote, "that I shall be well soon, but that it is most likely that some time will pass before I feel quite strong."

Dorothea Dix passed her time studying and writing more books—a book of hymns for children, religious meditations, a collection of short stories for children, and a book of poems and prose about flowers, which included such fascinating bits of information as "In Glamorganshire, England, it is yet a custom to strow the bed whereon a corpse rests with fragrant flowers."

Having to slow down didn't please her. "Dear Annie —Nothing seems to me so likely to make people unhappy in themselves and at variance with others as the habit of killing time," she wrote. It was during this time that Dorothea Dix allegedly got engaged and disengaged to Edward Bangs. This has never been proven and the only record of their romance is the stories passed on by family members. Francis Tiffany, who reviewed Dix's papers shortly after her death and wrote her biography, didn't mention Bangs. However, other authors who wrote about Dorothea Dix added the story about Bangs and implied that she never really recovered from her broken heart. That may be true, but then again it may not be. In deciding what to think, it's important for modern readers to know that in the letters Anne Heath kept, Dorothea Dix never mentioned being involved with Edward Bangs, let alone engaged to him.

In an effort to recover faster, Dorothea Dix left the harsh winter months in Boston for the warmer climate in Philadelphia, Pennsylvania and Alexandria, Virginia. There she stayed with relatives and spent her days reading, studying, walking, and collecting new specimens of flowers and plants. She also continued to follow the teachings of Dr. Channing to develop self-discipline and rise above her own imperfections. "Dear Annie—Do you know that I think the duty of self-examination one of the most difficult which we are called to perform ... Life is truly a state of discipline and of hourly trial ... It is dangerous to be neither hot nor cold," she wrote. Daily Dorothea Dix struggled to conquer her faults—selfishness, pride, anger, and vanity—and to perfect her virtues—humility, piety, self-denial, and service to others.

In 1927 Dr. Channing hired her to tutor his children for six months at their summer house in Portsmouth, Rhode Island. Years later, Mary, one of Channing's daughters, recalled Dorothea Dix as "tall and dignified, but stooped somewhat, very shy in manners and colored extremely when addressed. I think she was a very accomplished teacher, active and diligent herself very fond of natural history and botany. She enjoyed long rambles, always calling our attention to what was of interest in the world around us."

Three years later, Dr. Channing invited Dorothea Dix to accompany them to St. Croix, a lush tropical island in the Caribbean Sea. At first the hot climate laid her low. "How changed Miss Dix is!" Mary remarked. "She used always to be busy, and now she only says, 'Don't talk to me!' and throws herself on the bed twenty times a day." But before long Dix adjusted and threw herself into observing the island. She kept copious notes about everything—the culture, history, marine life, plants, religious practices, and geological formations. She collected specimens and filled many notebooks with her observations and studies.

Growing up in the north, Dorothea Dix had never had any actual experience with African slavery. What she saw on St. Croix made her indignant. "Disguise thyself, as thou wilt, still, slavery, still thou art a bitter draught," she wrote to a friend, Mrs. Torrey, "and human nature will not wear thy chains without cursing the ground for the enslaver's sake ... sure am I that a retribution will fall on the slave-merchant, the slave-holder, and their children to the fourth generation."

In the spring of 1831, Dorothea Dix returned to Boston from St. Croix in fine health. She felt restored and eagerly made plans to open another school in Dix Mansion. This time Madam Dix raised only one concern—would Dorothea Dix's health hold up this time?

Chapter Four

A MISSION FOR LIFE: 1831-1841

B̲y 1831, when Dorothea Dix opened The Dix Mansion Day and Boarding School, eight more states had joined the United States since the year she was born, including Louisiana, the first state west of the Mississippi River. Altogether there were twenty-four states, of which half allowed slavery and half prohibited it. A large part of what today is the United States, including what later became Texas and California, still belonged to Mexico. A smaller area, marked on maps as the Oregon Country, was claimed by both the United States and Britain.

All this would change as the United States entered a period of enormous growth and change. During a period of thirty years, the size of the country almost doubled, the population mushroomed from 11,000,000 people to 33,000,000, and a transportation system of roads, canals, and railroads was built, allowing goods and people to move around the huge country.

Andrew Jackson, the seventh president of the United States, was in office. A military hero and self-made success, Jackson was elected after the first name-calling and mud-slinging political campaign in American history — a fact that may seem strange to modern readers, who often don't know anything else except nasty political campaigns.

Change and new ideas were everywhere. The first covered wagons crossed the Rocky Mountains; the first horse-drawn buses carried passengers in New York City; Sylvester Graham developed the graham cracker; and the first successful women's magazine, *Godey's Lady's Book*, appeared. Americans from rural areas and immigrants from foreign countries flocked to the cities to work in factories.

Unfortunately, not all of the changes and ideas were good. Despite the fact that slavery was being abolished in other parts of the world (Britain made it illegal in 1833) thousands of African-Americans were still being bought and sold in the United States. In addition, this was the time in American history when the federal government and the states of Georgia, Mississippi, and Alabama joined forces to remove Native Americans from their homelands to unknown lands west of the Mississippi River. Thousands of Cherokee, Creek, Seminole, Choctaw, and Chickasaw Indians were forced to move, with thousands dying along the way. "To see the remnant of a once mighty people fettered and chained together forced to depart from the land of their fathers into a country unknown to them, is of itself sufficient to move the stoutest heart," wrote one newspaper reporter.

As has always been true in American history, there were people whose hearts were moved. And not only by the horrors of slavery and the treatment of Native Americans but by other social issues—war, alcohol abuse, poverty, and crime. In growing numbers, Americans started various efforts to reform society. William Lloyd Garrison started publishing *The Liberator*, a weekly newspaper dedicated to ending slavery in America. Other people formed temperance societies to stop the sale of alcohol and peace groups to stop war. Angelina and Sarah Grimké toured the country not only demanding the end of slavery but also insisting on the right of women to speak in public. "Are we aliens, because we are women?" Angelina Grimké asked in one speech. "Are we bereft of citizenship because we are mothers, wives and daughters of a mighty people?"

Although aware of the various reform movements and friends with many of the great reformers of the time, Dorothea Dix focused all her attention on starting her school. Like her first school, this one was a combination day and boarding school. The upstairs rooms in Dix Mansion were turned into dormitories. Classes were held downstairs in the large dining room where the long table was used for studying and eating. Dorothea Dix also reopened her charitable school in the barn for poor children.

"She fascinated me from the first," a student recalled years later, "as she had done many of my class before me. Next to my mother, I thought her the most beautiful woman I had ever seen. She was in the prime of her years, tall and of dignified carriage, head firmly shaped and set, with an abundance of soft, wavy brown hair."

Drawing on her love for nature, Dorothea Dix taught her students general science in addition to spelling, arithmetic, and English grammar. She also taught some Latin, and brought in another teacher to teach French. But the most important subject was character formation. Relentlessly Dix drilled her students in developing the habit of daily introspection. She instructed them to scrutinize their motives and behavior in order to overcome selfishness, pride, and vanity. A large seashell sat on the fireplace mantel into which pupils were instructed to drop letters recording their self-examinations and confessions of shortcomings.

"You wished me to be very frank with you and tell you my feelings," one student wrote. "I feel the need of some one to whom I can pour forth my feelings, they have been pent up so long. You may, perhaps, laugh when I tell you I have a *disease*, not of body but of mind. This is *unhappiness*. Can you tell me anything to cure it? If you can, I shall indeed be very glad."

Dorothea Dix's response to her student's plea is unknown; what is known is that night after night she stayed up past midnight writing answers full of advice to her students.

Dix's obsession with self-examination and self-improvement wasn't unusual. For this was a time in American history when people believed that social problems—poverty, crime, war—and individual shortcomings — drunkenness, laziness, greed — could be overcome if people tried hard enough and worked long enough to purify their thoughts and behavior. Like modern Americans who are obsessed with their physical health—eating the "right" foods and doing the "best" exercises — Dorothea Dix and many people like her were obsessed with their moral health. This concern was reflected in the magazines and books of their day, just as today a slew of magazines and books focuses on health and physical fitness.

"How little stress is to be laid on personal appearance," advised *Godey's Lady's Book*, a popular nineteenth century women's magazine, "It is always the mark of a weak mind, if not a bad heart, to hear a person praise and blame another on the ground alone that they are handsome or homely." Certainly very different advice than found in women's magazines published today, such as *Vogue* or *Cosmopolitan*!

For five years, Dorothea Dix drove herself hard. She achieved so much, including establishing her reputation as an excellent teacher and a successful author,

40

educating her brothers and seeing them start careers (Charles as a sailor and Joseph as a merchant), and accumulating enough money to support herself and take care of her mother. But it was too much. The pain in her side returned, her voice got weaker, and she started spitting up blood. This time the doctor feared Dorothea Dix might not recover. "Dear Annie —" she wrote, "For myself I feel that it is very possible I may never again enjoy the fragrances of Spring ..." Once again Dorothea Lynde Dix had to give up teaching.

In the hope that a total change would help her, Dorothea Dix's doctor ordered her to take a trip to England. Accompanied by two other couples, Dix boarded a ship on April 22, 1836. Never particularly fond of traveling by ship, she arrived in terrible shape and was confined to a hotel bed, unable to travel. Fortunately, good friends of William Ellery Channing, Mr. and Mrs. William Rathbone, who were prominent reformers in Britain, heard about her plight and took her to Greenbank, their home three miles outside of Liverpool. She was "an invalid," according to the Rathbones' son William, "a very, gentle and poetical and sentimental young lady, and in the then state of her health, without any appearance of mental energy or great power of character."

Recuperating at the Rathbones' home for eighteen months, Dorothea Dix enjoyed what she would always remember as the happiest time of her life. "You know I am ill," she wrote on October 1, 1836, to her friend Mrs. Samuel Torrey. "You must imagine me surrounded by every comfort, sustained by every tenderness that can cheer, blest in the continual kindness of the family in which Providence has placed me."

Slowly Dorothea Dix regained her strength. "Dear Annie —" she wrote in a letter dated January 25, 1837, "I have been very ill from the middle of November till the past week, but have just now less pain in the side, diminished cough, and, on the whole an accession of strength. This week, for the first time since September, the physician gave me permission to walk about the room several times daily. It is ten days since the last spitting of blood, and altogether I am quite comfortable, at least, I may say, happy and grateful for the manifold blessings of my condition."

Dorothea Dix returned to Boston in the autumn of 1837. Although she had recovered her health, her homecoming was difficult. Both her mother and grandmother had died during her absence. "Your mother's departure was so unexpected that even those in the room were totally unprepared; no sickness nor suffering, but a sudden summons to go to her rest after a life of suffering from a lingering disease," a friend informed her in a letter.

Madam Dix left Dorothea Dix a small inheritance that, along with the money from her books and her teaching, meant she had enough money to support herself without working. But what was life without work? What was her purpose in life? Dorothea agonized over these questions. "Dear Annie—Life is not to be expended in vain regrets," she wrote. "No day, no hour, comes but brings in its train work to be performed for some useful end—the suffering to be comforted, the wandering led home, the sinner reclaimed. Oh! how can any fold the hands to rest, and say to the spirit, 'Take thine ease, for all is well'!"

But Dorothea Dix's hands were folded. Alone, unsettled, restless, "depressed by the inactivity of my life," she journeyed from Virginia to New Hampshire taking care of personal business, visiting friends and relatives, reading and studying, and looking for "Some nobler purpose for which to labor, something which would fill the vacuum which I felt in my soul."

The weeks and months turned into years, as Dorothea Dix tried to find some meaning in her life. She read constantly, visited historic places, and struggled to regain her enthusiasm and energy. Depressed and absorbed with herself, she no longer signed "Thea" in her letters to Anne Heath. Now she was a more distant "D.L. Dix" or "D.L.D." In return, Anne Heath signed her letters "A.E. Heath" or "A.E.H." Despite the change in their signatures, Dorothea Dix still wrote "Dear Annie." Anne Heath began her letters with "My dear friend."

Finally, four years after her return from England, Dorothea Dix received a visit from John T.G. Nichols, a student at Harvard Divinity School. Nichols, as part of his training to become a minister, had been assigned to teach Sunday school to the women prisoners at the East Cambridge jail in Boston. After two sessions, Nichols decided that a mature woman, not a young man, should teach the women. His mother, a close friend of Dorothea Dix, suggested Nichols ask her advice as a renowned teacher.

"On hearing my account, Miss Dix said, after some deliberation, 'I will take them myself,'" Nichols recalled years later. "I protested her physical incapacity, as she was in feeble health. 'I shall be there next Sunday,' was her answer."

It was a cold, blustery day on March 28, 1841 when Dorothea Dix arrived at East Cambridge jail to teach Sunday school to the prisoners. But, first, with her characteristic curiosity, she insisted on having a tour of the jail. To her horror she discovered two indigent, or poverty-stricken, mentally ill women confined in cages made of rough boards—disheveled, shivering people whose only crime was their illness. No stove heated their bare, filthy pens. Why was there no heat, Dorothea asked the jailer. Because "lunatics" don't feel the cold, he replied.

Appalled and outraged, Dorothea launched a campaign to get stoves installed. When the jailer refused her repeated requests, she filed a legal case before the court and enlisted support from her friends, many of whom were such prominent politicians as Charles Sumner and Samuel Gridley Howe, the founder and director of the Perkins Institute for the Blind. Finally, in John Nichols' words, "Her request was granted. The cold rooms were warmed."

Were conditions as bad in other jails in Boston, Dorothea Dix wondered? Where else were indigent, mentally ill people confined? How were they treated? What were conditions like outside of Boston in the rest of Massachusetts? Determined to know, Dorothea Dix decided to find out firsthand. Never before in American history had any person—man or woman—set out to conduct such an extensive, systematic, and controversial investigation of a social condition. Dorothea Dix took it upon herself to embark upon what later historians would call "the first piece of social research ever conducted in America."

Dorothea Lynde Dix had found her purpose.

Chapter Five

GATHERING EVIDENCE: 1841-1842

As was her habit with all her endeavors, Dorothea Dix prepared herself thoroughly before setting out. Spending hours studying at the library, Dix was horrified at the extent of the mistreatment of mentally ill people. As late as 1815, the citizens of London could pay a penny to tour Bethlehem Hospital and gawk at seriously mentally ill people in tattered clothes rattling their chains, ranting, and raving. Along with the club-wielding guards, the sightseers considered it great fun to taunt and provoke the patients into greater states of frenzy. Less severely ill patients were dressed in black robes with white stars as a badge of identity and sent into the streets to beg for food.

From the beginning of history, Dorothea Dix discovered, superstition and ignorance had twisted people's attitudes toward mental illness. Ancient people thought evil spirits caused mental illness by possessing a person's mind; so they devised rituals, ceremonies, and foul potions to drive the evil spirits away. In some cases, ancient people removed a small circular section from the cranial bone at the top of a "possessed" person's skull to provide an opening for the demons to escape. People who survived this surgery—and some did

—were given the pieces of cranial bone, called ron-delles, to wear around their neck as an amulet.

Mental illness was also seen as divine punishment because a person had sinned—punishment that turned people into wild animals that needed to be chained, caged, and clubbed. Or it was seen as the work of the devil who turned people into witches—witches who had to be tortured and burned at the stake in order to protect society.

Mentally ill people with enough money or helpful friends or family, thus escaping being burned as witches or forgotten in cages and chains, still endured a variety of treatments. The so-called cures included purgings, or causing their bowels to empty out; emet-ics, or inducing vomiting; bleedings, or being cut and letting large amounts of blood drain out or having leeches put on their bodies to suck blood out; duck-ings, or being held under water to the point of passing out, but, hopefully, not dying; and whippings.

Throughout history there were a few enlightened people. Hippocrates, the author of more than sixty medical books and founder of a medical school in an-cient Greece, believed that health wasn't controlled by evil or divine spirits, but rather depended on the proper balance among four basic body substances, or humors — blood, phlegm, yellow bile, and black bile. According to Hippocrates, mental illness was caused by an imbalance in black bile. Soranus, another an-cient physician and who is considered the founder of gynecology and pediatrics, protested the treatment of mentally ill people. In writing about other doctors, So-ranus wrote, "... Rather than being themselves dis-posed to cure their patients, they seem to be in a state of delirium; they compare their patients to ferocious beasts whom they would subdue by the deprivation of food and by the torments of thirst. Misled without

46

doubt by this error, they advise that patients be cruelly chained, forgetting that their limbs might be injured ... they even advise bodily violence, like the use of the whip, as if such measures could force a return to reason; such treatment is deplorable and only aggravates the patient's condition ..."

Unfortunately these enlightened voices were few and it wasn't until the late 1700s that mentally ill people began to receive more humane treatment. Dr. Phillippe Pinel led the way in France. Appointed superintendent of Biceêtre, a notorious institution for insane men in Paris, Pinel believed that mental illness resulted from heredity and life experiences, not from evil spirits or divine punishment.

"Off with the chains!" Pinel ordered when he arrived at Bicêtre.

> "Away with these iron cages and brutal keepers! They make a hundred madmen when they cure one. There is another and a better way. The insane man is not an inexplicable monster. He is but one of ourselves, only a little more so. Underneath his wildest paroxysms there is a germ, at least, of rationality and of personal accountability. To believe in this, is to seek for it, stimulate it, build it up,— here lies the only way of delivering him out of the fatal bondage in which he is held."

The first patient Pinel freed from his chains was an English officer who had been imprisoned for forty years. "Oh, how beautiful," the officer exclaimed when he was led outside and turned his face toward the sun. Despite strenuous objections from many people, Pinel continued to free patients and practice what he called "moral treatment," which included clean, comfortable rooms, interesting activities, opportunities to exercise, intellectual stimulation, healthy food, and peaceful surroundings.

47

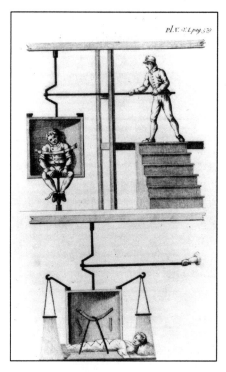

Whirling bed and whirling chair used to treat mentally ill people in the nineteenth century. People thought that the whirling motion relieved mental illness by increasing the blood supply to the brain. (Photo courtesy of National Library of Medicine.)

Nineteenth century mentally ill person bound with arm and leg restraints. (Photo courtesty of National Library of Medicine.)

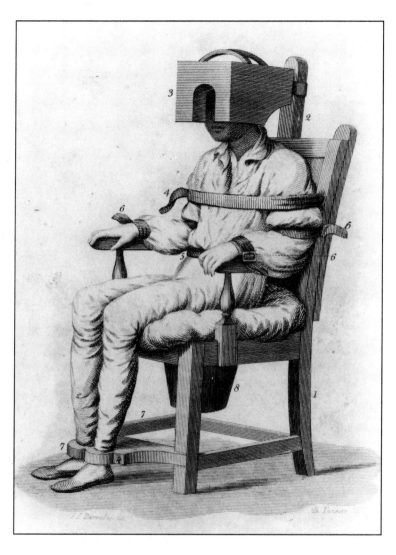

Tranquilizing chair used to treat mentally ill people in the nineteenth century. (Photo courtesy of National Library of Medicine.)

"The mentally sick," Pinel said, "far from being guilty people deserving of punishment are sick people whose miserable state deserves all the consideration that is due to suffering humanity. One should try with the most simple methods to restore their reasons."

Following Pinel's example, William Tuke established the York Retreat in England in 1796. Having met Tuke's son, Samuel, while she was in England, Dorothea remembered talking with him and the Rathbones about the importance of decent rooms, good food, relaxing activities, and proper medical care in the treatment of mental illness.

Upon learning that Dr. Luther V. Bell, the superintendent at the Mclean Asylum in Boston, a private hospital for mentally ill people, believed in moral treatment, Dorothea Dix went to talk with him and see what was going on at Mclean. Although she knew that few people could afford Mclean, Dix was inspired to see clean, comfortable, well-heated, lighted rooms, and talked with decently dressed patients, who were free to walk about, play billiards, ride horses, sew, and do other activities. Except in extreme cases, Dr. Bell explained, patients were not chained or locked in solitary confinement.

Dorothea Dix also talked with Horace Mann, who is known today as the great reformer for public education. It was Mann who had gotten the legislature to change the law that permitted sending mentally ill people to jail. Now, according to the law, "persons furiously mad" were to be committed to a "lunatic asylum." Equally important, Mann had also succeeded in getting legislators to appropriate money to build an asylum in Worcester, the State Lunatic Hospital, which opened in 1833. Another asylum, the Boston Lunatic Hospital, opened in 1839. But that was it—two hospitals run by the state, which were seriously overcrowded, and the

Mclean Asylum, which was small and expensive.

Dorothea Dix talked with Mann about an investigation he had conducted thirteen years earlier. By sending a questionnaire to town officials, Mann tried to find out what care was available for mentally ill people who didn't have family or money. Less than half of the officials responded, Mann explained, and those who did respond were probably not very truthful. Although he worried about Dorothea Dix's health, Mann applauded her plan to go see for herself how indigent mentally ill people were treated.

Dorothea Dix set out in the spring and spent two years gathering evidence. Traveling by wagon and stagecoach, she visited every place in Massachusetts where poor, mentally ill people were kept — almshouses, jails, workhouses, and private homes in which lunatics and idiots (lunatics meaning mentally ill people and idiots meaning mentally retarded people) were boarded out by town officials to the lowest bidder. With the same diligence and thoroughness that she had exhibited before — whether teaching in Boston or observing every aspect of life on St. Croix—Dorothea Dix kept detailed notes about what she saw.

In one town after another she meticulously recorded her discoveries in a notebook. In Danvers she found a young woman:

> "... clinging to, or beating upon, the bars of her caged apartment, the contracted size of which afforded space only for increasing accumulation of filth—a foul spectacle; there she stood, with naked arms and disheveled hair; the unwashed frame invested with fragments of unclean garments; the air so extremely offensive, though ventilation was afforded on all sides save one, that it was not possible to remain beyond a few moments without retreating for recovery to the outward air. Irritation of body, produced by utter filth and exposure, incited

51

her to the horrid process of tearing off her skin by inches. Her face, neck, and person were thus disfigured by hideousness. She held up a fragment just rent off to my exclamation of horror, the mistress replied, 'Oh, we can't help it. Half the skin is off sometimes ...'"

In Wayland she saw a man:

"... caged in a woodshed, fully exposed on a public road. Confinement and cold have so affected his limbs that he is often powerless to rise ..."

In Shelburne she:

"... was conducted into the yard, where was a small building of rough boards imperfectly joined. All was still, save now and then a low groan. The person who conducted me tried, with a stick, to rouse the inmate; I entreated her to desist; the twilight of the place making it difficult to discern anything within the cage; there at last I saw a human being, partially extended, cast upon his back amidst a mass of filth, the sole furnishing, whether for comfort or necessity, which the place afforded; there he lay, ghastly, with unturned, glazed eyes and fixed gaze, heavy breathing, interrupted only by faint groans ..."

Always probing, Dorothea Dix talked to the keepers. In Fitchburg she asked the keeper of an almshouse why he didn't take a young man, confined to a cell, outside for exercise and fresh air. Admitting that he had thought of that before, the keeper said, "I've proposed getting from the blacksmith an iron collar and chain; then I can have him out by the house."

"An iron collar and chain!" Dix responded.

"Yes, I had a cousin up in Vermont, crazy as a wildcat, and I got a collar made for him, and he liked it."

"Liked it! How did he manifest his pleasure?"

"Why, he left off trying to run away," the keeper explained.

In Newton she found an old man chained to a bunk in a woodshed. Observing that he had stumps because his feet had been amputated after they had frozen one winter, Dorothea Dix asked the keeper why he was chained. "Oh, he can crawl, and when he gets mad he might do some damage," the keeper replied.

Not all keepers were so insensitive and ignorant. Some provided decent care. Others wanted to, but told Dix they didn't have enough money.

At every stop, Dorothea Lynde Dix comforted the mentally ill people she saw. With her brown hair parted in the middle, smoothed down to a soft curve in front of each ear and braided into a bun at the back of her finely shaped head, Dorothea Dix didn't hesitate to lift her long skirt and walk into muddy and foul places. Striking in her appearance, with clear skin, a long slender neck, firm chin, wide mouth with her lower lip slightly larger than the upper, narrow nose, high cheekbones, and blue-grey eyes with pupils so large that sometimes her eyes looked black, Dorothea Dix carried herself with authority. The sound of her voice added to her remarkable presence. It was, "Sweet, rich, low, perfect in enunciation and every tone pervaded with blended love and power," according to one account.

Dorothea Dix spent hours talking with people who had been labeled "lunatics ... idiots ... furiously mad" and locked away in dreadful places. "Heavenly visits," is what one inmate called Dorothea Dix's visits. And she didn't forget them after she left. With the help of her friends, Dorothea Dix sent magazines and books and left boxes of clothes at jails and almshouses.

Time and time again Dix silenced her outrage and suppressed her urge to break the chains. She disciplined herself to keep on gathering evidence: to keep on uncovering one horror after another and to keep on traveling over rutted and rough roads, riding noisy and dirty trains, and sleeping wherever she could—sometimes in a narrow, hard bed in a small inn, other times sitting up in a chair in waiting rooms, or still other times bouncing on the stiff seat of a wagon or coach or train as she moved from village to town.

Dorothea Dix persisted because she had a plan—a plan larger than just getting stoves installed as she had in the East Cambridge jail. She was going to get indigent mentally ill people out of chains and cages and into decent state hospitals. But first she had to get existing hospitals expanded and new hospitals built, and that required approval from the governor and legislators. Approval Dorothea Dix was determined to get, regardless of the fact that, as a woman, she couldn't even vote.

Chapter Six

PRESENTING HER CASE: 1843

Undaunted by the fact that she was a retired schoolteacher in frail health without wealth or power to support her cause, Dorothea Dix completed her investigation and planned her next move. In consultation with her friends, Dix decided to present her findings in the form of a Memorial, a document that presents facts and requests action, to the Massachusetts Legislature. Her friend Dr. Samuel Gridley Howe, a member of the legislature, offered to present it personally and introduce a bill to build new hospitals.

Gathering together two years of vivid memories and graphic notes, Dorothea Dix wrote powerful prose designed to move the most apathetic politician:

> "GENTLEMEN ... I respectfully ask to present this Memorial ... I shall be obliged to speak with great plainness, and to reveal many things revolting to the taste, and from which my woman's nature shrinks with peculiar sensitiveness. But truth is the highest consideration. *I tell what I have seen*—painful and shocking as the details often are—that from them you may feel more deeply this imperative obligation which lies upon you to prevent the possibility of a repetition or continuance of such outrages upon humanity ... I come to present the strong claim of

suffering humanity. I come to place before the Legislature of Massachusetts the condition of the miserable, the desolate, the outcast. I come as the advocate of the helpless, forgotten, insane and idiotic men and women; of beings sunk to a condition from which the most unconcerned would start with real horror; of beings wretched in our prisons, and more wretched in our almshouses ... If my pictures are displeasing, coarse, and severe, my subjects, it must be recollected, offer no tranquil, refined, or composing features. The condition of human beings, reduced to the extremest states of degradation and misery, cannot be exhibited in softened language ...

"I proceed, gentlemen, briefly to call your attention to the *present* state of insane persons confined within this Commonwealth, in *cages, closets, cellars, stalls, pens! Chained, naked, beaten with rods, and lashed* into obedience! In illustration of my subject, I offer the following extracts from my Notebook and Journals: *Lincoln*: A woman in a cage. *Medford*: One idiotic subject chained, and one in a close stall for seventeen years. *Pepperell*: One often doubly chained, hand and foot ... *Granville*: One often closely confined, now losing the use of his limbs from want of exercise. *Charlemont*: One man caged. *Savoy*: One man caged ... *Dedham*: One of the subjects is supposed curable. The overseers of the poor have declined giving her a trial at the hospital, as I was informed, on account of expenses ..."

She also included an example of what humane treatment could do:

"Some may say these things cannot be remedied; these furious maniacs are not to be raised from these base conditions. I *know* they are; could give *many* examples; let one suffice. A young woman, a pauper in a distant town ... A cage, chains, and the whip were the agents for her, united with harsh tones and profane. Annually, with others (the town's poor) she was put up at auction, and bid off at the lowest price which was declared for her. One year not long past, an old man came forward in the number of applicants for the poor wretch; he was taunted and ridiculed. What would he and his old wife do with such a mere beast? 'My wife say yes,' replied he, 'and I shall take her.' She was given to his charge: he conveyed her home; she was washed, neatly dressed, and placed in a decent bedroom, furnished for comfort and opening into the kitchen. How altered her condition! As yet the *chains* were not off. The first week she was somewhat restless, at times violent, but the quiet ways of the old people wrought a change; she received her food decently; forsook acts of violence, and no longer uttered blasphemous or indecent language. After a week the chain was lengthened, and she was received as a companion in the kitchen. Soon she engaged in trivial employments. 'After a fortnight,' said the old man. 'I knocked off the chains and made her a free woman.' She is at times excited, but not violently, they are careful of her diet, they keep her very clean, she calls them father and mother. Go there now, and you will find her 'clothed,' and though not perfectly in her 'right mind' so far restored as to be a safe and comfortable inmate."

"Men of Massachusetts," Dorothea Dix wrote in conclusion, "I beg, I implore, I demand pity and protection for these of my suffering, outraged sex. Become the benefactors of your race, the just guardians of the solemn rights you hold in trust ... I do most sincerely hope that more permanent provisions will be made for the pauper insane by the State . . . Gentlemen, I commit to you this sacred cause. Your action upon this subject will affect the present and future condition of hundreds and of thousands . . ."

Respectfully submitted.
D.L. Dix
85 Mt. Vernon Street, Boston January 1843

57

Dorothea Lynde Dix in a portrait taken from a daguerreo-type in the early 1840s. (Photo courtesy of National Archives.)

"I presented your Memorial this morning," Dr. Samuel Gridley Howe wrote in a note to Dix. "When I look back upon the time when you stood hesitating and doubting upon the brink of the enterprise you have so bravely and nobly accomplished, I cannot but be impressed with the lesson of courage and hope which you have taught even to the strongest men ... You are pleased to overrate the importance of my efforts. I can reply that if I *touch off* the piece, it will be you who *furnish the ammunition.*"

The reaction to Dix's Memorial was intense—"Lies! Libelous! Sensationalism!" local officials and almshouse keepers and jail wardens charged. All across Massachusetts people denied Dorothea's charges. The state of her mental health was questioned. Newspaper editors blasted her in articles and editorials. Reports were quickly issued that painted a different picture. Dorothea Dix was stunned but resolute. Dr. Howe was furious. Her friends rallied to support her. Charles Sumner, the popular speaker and statesman, visited four almshouses that Dix had described in her Memorial and wrote an article in the *Boston Courier*, "... I am obliged to add that it accords most literally with the condition of things at the time of my visit ... The correctness with which Miss Dix has described the four almshouses which I have seen leads me to place entire confidence in her descriptions."

Despite the furor, Dorothea Dix didn't back down. She wrote notes and met privately with legislators to plead her case. She reassured local officials that she wasn't attacking them personally. In addition to Sumner and Howe, she got public support from other prominent people. In short, she conducted what today would be considered a highly sophisticated public relations campaign. Slowly the tide turned. Citizens and politicians alike began admitting the truth of Dorothea

Dix's charges. Finally, by a large majority even, the legislature appropriated money to expand the hospital at Worcester.

Dorothea Dix had won.

During her investigation in Massachusetts, Dorothea Dix had frequently crossed the borders of adjoining states — New York, Rhode Island, Connecticut — and seen enough to know that they needed a thorough investigation too. In addition, as news of her victory spread, concerned citizens from other parts of the country wrote and asked her to come.

Clearly Dorothea Lynde Dix's crusade had just begun.

Chapter Seven

INTREPID TRAVELER: 1843-1846

"I have traveled over ten thousand miles in the last three years. I have visited 18 penitentiaries, 100 county jails and houses of correction, more than 500 almshouses and other institutions, besides hospitals and houses of reform," Dorothea Dix wrote to Mrs. Rathbone in England in early 1845. "Jail to jail," she wrote in another letter, "prison to poorhouse, through almost trackless forests, over mountains, through swamps. Often the way lies through a wilderness, traced by slight cuts on trees, houses fourteen or twenty miles apart, if they can be called houses, single rooms of logs and a stone chimney. Four nights out of nine able to find such rest as I might in two chairs, wide chinks between logs. Cold."

Women didn't travel often or far in Dorothea Dix's day. And they certainly didn't travel alone. Yet Dorothea Dix did. Crisscrossing every state from Maine to Louisiana, Georgia to Illinois, and into Canada, she endured difficult and dangerous conditions to continue her crusade. Her letters to Anne Heath and other friends as she traveled through Pennsylvania painted a vivid picture of her journeys:

"August. Lancaster from Philadelphia. Overseer of the poor in bad health and temper. Changed mood when he learned my name. Went to poor house, stayed four hours. He asked me to write for their paper. I objected, 'No one would know me.' 'You are mistaken. Every man and woman in Lancaster, if not our state, knows who you are.' Had to write ... Stage for Bedford, 13½ hours hard riding. Poor horse. Set off a little past midnight to cross mountains, reached top of Alleghenies (mountains) at daylight. Wagon to Somerset ... stage, three hours to Mt. Pleasant. Had to leave at once because it went only once a week. Dreadful night's journey ... Saw almshouse and jail, horrible. Wrote four pages ... thirty-four hours without stop except to change horses ... boat to Pittsburgh ... Meadville ... Erie ... to Warren, no road, would take more than fifty miles horseback, cannot attempt that, had to take long route through New York by Jamestown."

To get to Franklin, Dorothea Dix wrote in one letter, she had a choice between taking:

"A skiff sixty-nine miles down the Allegheny or a wagon without springs over a road for which I have no terms sufficiently graphic. Wagon rejected, I proceeded to the banks, where I discovered an old waterman, astride upon a drift log half under water, chewing a cud and whittling away on a pine stick. Hair uncombed, face unshaved. Took myself at two the following morning to this precious vehicle and after 19 hours steady travel found myself with the U.S. mails in Franklin ... Such roads by which I reached the interior country! Four carriages broke down. Why the horses did not is a wonder. The last carriage I hired in Indiana to convey me to Ebersburg has seen hard service. I suggested to my driver to proceed with more care over the rocks, but he graciously responded he 'knowed how to drive my horse and bein' as he had a woman aboard he'd been a-comin' slow as —' His eloquence was abridged by the creaking of the springs. Down one came crushed and broken. A dilemma. There seemed to be no alternative for me but to walk to Ebersburg, five long miles, or spend the night in the forest. The last bright beams of the sun touched the tops of the gigantic trees. The faint notes of the lingering birds were heard at longer intervals when an equestrian appeared, came nigh, and paused to consider our disaster, but he did more. He had a fine lead horse and said, 'If the lady will walk a quarter of a mile we may borrow a saddle, and she is welcome to either of my horses.'

"It was no time for demurs. I walked to the log hut, a saddle was borrowed, the steed suffered me to mount, and we entered the first town on Cambria County at dark. I alighted at the hotel and took leave, sending my saddle home and later getting my luggage from the dilapidated vehicle."

A broken spring wasn't the only thing that could go wrong with a carriage or stagecoach or wagon. All too often, wheels fell off, axles broke, and harnesses tore. Since most drivers didn't carry repair kits, Dorothea Dix, with her usual practical approach to life, packed her own kit containing carpenter's tools, nails, rope, leather for patching, and a can of axle grease. Few roads were paved with macadam (a mixture of crushed stones and tar); most were simply made with loose gravel, packed earth, or logs laid sideways (called corduroy roads). To get to remote villages, Dorothea frequently traveled over roads that were nothing more than two tracks through the forest.

Mud so deep that the wheels sank in up to the axles, potholes, ice, and streams without bridges also made travel treacherous. "I have encountered nothing so dangerous as river fords," Dorothea Dix wrote during a trip through North Carolina. "I crossed the Yadkin where it was three fourths of a mile wide, rough

63

bottom, often in places rapid currents; the water always up to the bed of the carriage, and sometimes flowing in. The horses rested twice on sand-bars. A few miles beyond the river, having just crossed a deep branch two hundred yards wide, the axletree of the carriage broke and away rolled one of the back wheels."

During this same trip to North Carolina, a newspaper reporter asked Dorothea Dix if she was ever afraid. "I am naturally timid," Dix replied, "but in order to carry out my purposes, I know that it is necessary to make sacrifices and encounter dangers." She then went on to tell how, during a journey through Michigan, her carriage was stopped by a robber.

> "I said to him, with as much self-possession as I could command, 'Are you not ashamed to rob a woman? I have but little money, and that I want to defray my expenses in visiting prisons and poor-houses and occasionally in giving to objects of charity. If you have been unfortunate, are in distress and in want of money, I will give you some.' While thus speaking to him I discovered his countenance changing, and he became deathly pale. 'My God,' he exclaimed, 'that voice!' and immediately told me that he had been in the Philadelphia penitentiary and had heard me lecturing to some of the prisoners in an adjoining cell. He then desired me to pass on, and expressed deep sorrow at the outrage he had committed. But I drew out my purse, and said to him, 'I will give you something to support you until you can get into honest employment.' He declined, at first, taking anything, until I insisted on his doing so, for fear he might be tempted to rob some one else before he could get into honest employment."

Wherever she could, Dorothea Dix saved time and traveled by train. Although faster than carriages, stage-coaches, and wagons, trains weren't much safer or more comfortable. Derailments were frequent, collisions with cows that wandered onto the tracks were common, and, all too often, sparks from the wood-burning furnace in the locomotive started fires in the fields along the tracks. By the end of a train trip Dix's eyes were red and her voice sore from the soot, cinders, and dust that seeped into the passenger car where she sat on a hard seat.

She also traveled by steamboats. Up and down such great rivers as the Ohio, Wabash, Monongahela, and Mississippi, Dorothea Dix traveled to Savannah, Georgia; Cincinnati, Ohio; St. Louis, Missouri; New Orleans, Louisiana; Memphis, Tennessee; Little Rock, Arkansas; and Alton, Illinois.

On the most elegant steamboat on the Mississippi River, Dorothea Dix had a six by six-foot stateroom with a narrow shelf for a berth, a pitcher filled with cold river water in which the silt had settled, a tin basin, and a commode—a box with a hole in the top over a chamber pot. Flies, mosquitoes, and an occasional rat kept her company. On more modest steamboats, Dix and the other passengers shared quarters with worn bed sheets, pillows filled with corn husks, and a row of pitchers, basins, and, for those few people who took care of their teeth, a communal toothbrush on a chain.

The best boats offered incredible food. Dinner would include one soup, six kinds of boiled meats, five types of fish, eleven entrées such as spiced pig's head, nine roasts, five kinds of game, potatoes, rice, corn, fifteen pastries and desserts, fruits, nuts, and lots of whiskey and rum. The worst boats—"the very filthliest of all filthy old rat-traps I ever traveled in," in the words of one traveler—offered salt pork, hominy, rice, beans, and black coffee.

Loaded with sugar, salt, coffee, hardware, and dry

goods for trips south, and with cotton, tobacco, pork, and lard for trips north, steamboats encountered various dangers such as submerged branches that tore holes in the boat's bottom, hidden sandbars that stopped a boat fast, low water that slowed it down, and explosions in its boilers. "We had a narrow escape from loss of life and boat three nights since," Dix wrote to her brother Joseph. "The pilot at the wheel fell into a fit, and the boat went berserk, striking rocks and breaching the wheelhouse. A boy with the pilot was too terrified to give assistance. The mate dashed for the pilot house but could not enter, the pilot having fallen against the door. We were detained some hours to repair the damage."

Cholera and malaria were common diseases, and Dorothea Dix spent many nights sitting by the bedside of deathly ill passengers. "Up again from malarial fever," she, in her matter-of-fact way, wrote to her friends about the state of her own health. Always prepared, Dorothea Dix added a first-aid kit to her valise.

Her valise also contained an abundance of stationery, notebooks, pencils, pens, and ink, for Dorothea Dix was always writing, whether it was detailed notes about how prisoners and indigent mentally ill people were treated, articles intended to change public attitudes about mental illness, or letters — thousands and thousands of letters. Letters to politicians seeking their vote; to philanthropists soliciting contributions that included money, books, and musical instruments for patients; to superintendents of hospitals providing or requesting information; and to her friends, whom she looked to for encouragement and support. "I must have sympathy just now. I need calmness. I am exhausted under this perpetual effort and exercise of fortitude," she wrote to a friend, who replied by inviting Dix to come for a rest.

Writing under difficult conditions, Dorothea Dix's

66

The Bible she always carried with her on her travels around the country. On the inside her initials were engraved in leather. (Photos courtesy of the Trenton Psychiatric Hospital.)

handwriting was frequently hard to read. Dr. Isaac Ray, her good friend and superintendent at Butler Hospital, reported that he and his wife spent most of one evening decipering one of her letters: "We succeeded with one exception ... I will copy the characters and perhaps you may be able to recognize them ..."

When writing her memorials, however, Dix's handwriting was clear and firm. Since her victory in Massachusetts, Dorothea Dix had written memorials to the legislatures of New York, New Jersey, Pennsylvania, Kentucky, and the parliament of Canada. All were successful — existing hospitals in Utica, New York and Lexington, Kentucky were being expanded and new hospitals were being built in Trenton, New Jersey; Harrisburg, Pennsylvania; Green River County, Kentucky; and Toronto, Canada. In addition, she was responsible for improving conditions in numerous penitentiaries and almshouses. Each victory spurred her on. "Dear Annie — Heaven has greatly blessed my labors, and I feel truly and more that a leading Providence defines my path in the dark valleys of the world," she wrote.

But three years of nonstop efforts finally proved to be too much. The stress of her travels and recurrent attacks of malaria caught up with Dorothea Dix and in September 1846 she collapsed in Columbus, Ohio. In a letter to Anne Heath, she wrote:

"My robe of life is travel-worn,
And dusty with the dusty way;
It bears the mark of many a storm
And marks of many a toilsome day
The morning shower, the damp nights dews
Have lent their dark discoloring hues."

Once again illness stopped Dorothea Lynde Dix.

Would she have to quit? Give up her crusade just as she had had to give up her schools? And resign herself to life as an invalid?

Chapter Eight

RELENTLESS CRUSADER: 1846-1848

At the time of her collapse, Dorothea Dix was writing memorials to the legislatures of Illinois and Tennessee. She also had plans to survey Alabama, Mississippi, and North Carolina. This was no time to be bedridden. But now Dorothea Dix couldn't even hold a pen. For eight weeks she suffered with fever and severely inflamed lungs. Racked with chills and exhausted from coughing up blood, she struggled to survive.

"I encounter nothing, which a determined will, created by the necessities of the cause I advocate, does not enable me to vanquish," she had written to her close friend George Emerson three years earlier while onboard the steamer *Chautauqua*, traveling on Lake Erie to Barcelona, New York. Now, it seemed that illness, once again, would stop her ... be something she couldn't overcome ... make her give up her crusade as she had given up her schools.

However, this time was different. This time Dorothea Dix had a purpose; a purpose that she couldn't give up. Slowly she started to get better. "Dear Annie—I could not sit up for one hour at a time," she wrote. "Now I sit up most of the day, can walk below stairs unassisted." By December she was off again, and on

January 16, 1847 her Memorial to the Illinois legislature was presented in Springfield, Illinois.

As was her custom, Dorothea Dix stayed in Springfield after her Memorial was presented to lobby the legislators. Presenting the Memorial was one thing; making sure that the politicians passed a bill to expand and build hospitals was another. Dix used the same strategy in every state—she studied the list of politicians and learned everything she could about them. Were they sympathetic to her cause? Would they vote to appropriate money for a hospital? Could they influence other legislators? Then she invited them to discuss her memorial with her.

Determined not to jeopardize her cause by offending the prevailing standards of ladylike behavior (any more than she already had by traveling alone, writing memorials, and demanding change), Dorothea Lynde Dix didn't storm the halls of the legislature or confront politicians in public. Instead, she discreetly arranged to have a room or a corner set aside for her in a library, in a friend's house, or in the parlor of her hotel or boardinghouse. There she invited legislators to meet her. Day and night Dorothea Dix presented her case to small and large groups of legislators (all men—women couldn't vote then, let alone serve in the legislature).

Head erect, back straight, eyes unwavering, she discussed her findings and recommendations. Then she asked the legislators to vote to build hospitals for indigent mentally ill people, to appropriate taxpayers' money. It wasn't "charity," she explained. Not at all. Rather it was their duty "to respond to the claims of humanity, and to acknowledge the demands of justice."

Ridiculous, some legislators responded. During Dix's campaign in New Jersey, one legislator proposed that they appropriate money to escort her out of the state. In another state a legislator suggested that they just vote to cover over the cages and plant grass. (Hostile and sarcastic legislators didn't bother Dorothea Dix as much as the ones who praised her and her work but when it came time to vote on providing decent care, voted "no.")

Undeterred, Dorothea Dix kept up her efforts. She wrote numerous newspaper articles, gave many interviews, and talked to countless numbers of civic leaders and ordinary citizens.

"You cannot imagine the labor of conversing and convincing," she wrote to her friend Harriet Hare after her successful campaign in New Jersey. But it was worth it. Time and time again, the depth of Dorothea Dix's knowledge, passion of her commitment, and strength of her personality won converts to her cause.

"Last evening a rough county member," she told Harriet Hare, "who had announced in the House that the 'wants of the insane in New Jersey were all humbug' and who came to overwhelm me with arguments, after listening an hour and a half with wonderful patience to my details and to principles of treatment, suddenly moved into the middle of the parlor, and thus delivered himself: 'Ma'am, I bid you good-night! I do not want, for my part, to hear anything more; the others can stay if they want to. I am convinced; you've conquered me out and out; I shall vote for the hospital.'"

Finally, in March the Illinois legislature appropriated money to build the Illinois State Hospital for the Insane in Jacksonville. Tennessee was next, where she was even invited to present her Memorial to the legislature herself—an unprecedented opportunity for a woman—which Dorothea Dix accepted. As she walked to the podium, the men rose to their feet and applauded her.

Dorothea never took shortcuts. In each state she conducted a thorough investigation, talked to doctors, judges, keepers, prisoners, and mentally ill people,

71

and enlisted the support of newspaper editors and politicians. Everywhere she went she developed a network of friends—from governors to ordinary citizens, and even people who didn't approve of her crusade. Such was the case with Louisa Hall, the wife of Reverend Edward Hall, who had begged Dorothea to come investigate conditions in Rhode Island. Louisa Hall wasn't looking forward to Dorothea Dix's visit. She didn't approve of what she considered Dix's unladylike behavior. However, "One look at that calm, gentle face had its effect," Louisa Hall recalled years later, "Then only a word of sweet ladylike apology in a sweet low voice, and I began to feel the gift she had. I was mending my boy's socks, and she quietly took one up and began darning with a skillful hand ... For two hours we sat together and not one word about the insane or her 'mission.' After dinner she said to my husband, 'Now I am at your service.'"

Undeniably sweet and gentle, Dorothea Dix did whatever it took to provoke public awareness and discussion, including expressing scathing criticism, as unladylike as it was. Her tart tongue was obvious in a newspaper article she wrote about the plight of Abram Simmons, whom she discovered chained to the floor of a stone dungeon in Rhode Island. "The people of that region profess the Christian religion," she concluded the article, "and it is even said they have adopted some forms and ceremonies which they call worship. It is not probable, however, that they address themselves to poor Simmons's God. Their worship, mingling with the prayers of agony which he shrieks forth from his dreary abode, would make strange discord in the ear of that Almighty Being, in whose keeping sleeps the vengeance due to all his wrongs."

Through her efforts Dorothea Dix was changing the way people thought about mental illness. "It is time that people should have learnt that to be insane is not to be disgraced; that sickness is not to be ranked with crime; and that mental disability is almost invariably the result of mere bodily ailment," she repeated in her articles, memorials, and conversations. Equally important, she insisted, was the fact that mental illness was curable: "The malady of insanity, when brought under *early efficient treatment*, is, except there be organic disease, equally manageable and curable as a fever or a cold." The power of her persuasiveness was proven each time a legislature responded positively to her Memorials. With one major exception, Dorothea Dix always got at least part of what she asked for sooner or later. Altogether she was responsible for the building or expansion of thirty-two hospitals for mentally ill people, fifteen training schools for mentally retarded people, and improvements at numerous almshouses and penitentiaries.

Turning down request after request to have institutions named after her, she finally allowed two hospitals to be named after her beloved grandfather — Dix Hill Hospital in Raleigh, North Carolina (today called the Dorothea Dix Hospital) and Dixmont Hospital near Pittsburgh, Pennsylvania (today the hospital is closed). Despite her desire to avoid personal glory, Dorothea quickly became famous. Babies were named after her, governors invited her to stay with them, and awards were sent to her. State legislatures adopted resolutions honoring her, such as this one, which she received beautifully inscribed and framed:

"That the thanks of this General Assembly and of the People of Tennessee are due and are hereby most respectfully tendered to Miss D. L. Dix for her very valuable efforts bestowed on a project to establish an institution for the better security, comfort, and improvement of those unfortunate classes of our community known as idiots and lunatics and that her disinterested benevolence, sublime charity, and unmixed philanthrophy shall engage alike the gratitude and admiration of our State."

Throughout her life, Dorothea Dix kept close watch on institutions throughout the country. No detail escaped her. "A few Brackets in yr. [your] reception rooms — with Books or flower-vases of pretty shapes and harmonizing colors—which need be tasteful rather than costly," she wrote in a letter to one hospital superintendent. "A few nice articles on the mantle-pieces and tables, etc. Excuse suggestions ... Will you let me add the *suggestion* only that perhaps a few degrees higher temperature than is usually supplied for the patient may be conducive of much increased comfort. Is not 68 degrees rather low for feeble people of impaired health?—and rather thinly clad?"

"To have Miss Dix suddenly arrive at your asylum and find anything neglected or amiss, was considerably worse than an earthquake," wrote Dr. Isaac Ray. "Not that she said anything on the spot, but one felt something ominous suspended in the very air."

After a surprise visit from Dix, Dr. John W. Sawyer, who followed Ray as superintendent at Butler Hospital, wrote to Ray, "We have recently had a visit from Miss Dix, who criticized some things more severly than I have been accustomed to hear and left me a little discouraged."

To which Dr. Ray replied, "She often censures without good judgment [meaning tact], but has generally a basis for her censures."

Enlisting her friends and organizing concerned citizens, Dorothea Dix provided a variety of items for hospitals and prisons throughout the country—books, bowling alleys, artwork, plants, horses and carriages, and new devices called magic lanterns that projected slides of beautifully painted pictures on the wall. And she worked fast. "Finding the convicts unsupplied with any books except the Bible," reported a warden at a prison in Alabama she visited, "... and being unable to discover any law authorizing the same to be furnished at the expense of the State, the Inspector, soon after her departure, received some two or three hundred volumes of works, which were donated by her to the use and improvement of convicts ..."

Dorothea Dix involved everyone she met in her crusade, including the children of her friends. Why don't you donate this toy or that one, she would say. Knowing that she was irresistible, the children quickly learned to hide their *favorite* toy, or picture, or game before she arrived. Enormously fond of children, Dorothea Dix delighted in playing puzzles and word games with them. Her pockets and bag were always stuffed with scraps of paper — thin blue pieces, lined white pieces, and torn-off corners of stationery — on which she had written the latest puzzle with the answer carefully printed underneath. Hundreds of these puzzles were found in her belongings after her death, such as: "Taking the human head for the subject what part therein do you find in a potato? (eye) What part of the green leaf upon a tree? (veins & vessels) What part in a corn patch? (ears) What flowers? (iris and tu lips)."

Of all her hospitals, Dorothea Dix was particularly fond of the New Jersey State Lunatic Asylum in Trenton. It was the first totally new hospital built as a result of her memorial. Her "first-born child," she called it.

Dix was asked to help pick the site and design the building. A firm believer in moral treatment, which stressed peaceful surroundings, Dorothea Dix selected a spot on a high hill with a beautiful view of the valley and the Delaware River below. She consulted with the architect about designing a long stone building with white columns, a majestic dome, and bright spacious rooms. No detail escaped her attention, "In the patients' rooms the *door* should open *opposite* the window—the *head* of the bed be placed against the outer wall, facing the door,—both that the *light* may not strike directly upon the patients' eyes in bed, and that the door need not open at the *head* of the bed," she commented after reviewing one set of plans.

Ever since Dix Mansion had been sold after Madam Dix's death, Dorothea Dix had lived with friends and relatives or in hotels and boarding houses. Now a room with a wonderful view at the Trenton hospital was set aside for her use. Finally she had a home. But she wouldn't be there often. Not now. Not when she was about to undertake her grand plan.

New Jersey State Lunatic Asylum—the hospital Dorothea Dix called her "first born child." Dix's apartment was located in the dome above the main building with the columns. The main building was destroyed by fire in the 1970s and rebuilt. The view of the valley from Dorothea Dix's apartment was spectacular, and it remains so today. Trees and bushes planted from cuttings Dix collected are still growing in magnificent splendor. (Photo courtesy of the Trenton Psychiatric Hospital, Trenton, New Jersey.)

Chapter Nine

A GRAND PLAN: 1848-1854

The federal government owned lots of land—millions of acres. It was land that it had fought wars to get; land that it had bought from other countries; and land that it had gotten through treaty agreements with other countries. Most of the land was unoccupied—except by Native Americans, whose rights to the land weren't taken seriously. Since the land, or public land as it was called, belonged to the federal government, not to a particular state, company, or individual, Congress had the right to decide what to do with it.

For years, Congress had been selling public lands in small plots for $1.25 to $2.00 an acre to settlers or in large blocks to speculators, who then subdivided it into farms or towns and resold it at a profit. By the time Dorothea Dix started her crusade, more and more people wanted public lands—developers, farmers, railroad companies, and corporations. In addition, Senators Henry Clay from Kentucky and Thomas Hart Benton from Missouri wanted Congress to transfer large pieces of public lands to the states so that schools or roads could be built.

Why not set aside public lands for the care of the "poor and helpless," Dorothea Dix wondered? What a

grand plan! She discussed her idea with her friends—
George Emerson, Horace Mann, Anne Heath, Harriet
Hare, Drs. Luther Bell and John Butler, and her
brother Joseph (her brother Charles had recently died
at sea). A wonderful idea, they said, but it can't be
done. Of course, Dorothea Dix refused to believe that.
"They say nothing can be done here," she had once
written to Harriet Hare, "I reply, 'I know no such word
in the vocabulary I adopt!'"

On June 23, 1848, Dorothea Lynde Dix's grand
plan, a memorial to the United States Congress asking
for 5,000,000 acres of public lands, was presented.

> "... I have myself seen *more than nine thousand*
> *idiots, epileptics, and insane in these United*
> *States, destitute of appropriate care and protec-*
> *tion*; and of the vast and miserable company,
> sought out in jails, in poorhouses, and in private
> dwellings, there have been hundreds,—nay, rather
> thousands,—bound with galling chains, bowed be-
> neath fetters and heavy iron balls attached to drag
> chains, lacerated with ropes, scourged with rods,
> and terrified beneath storms of profane exertions
> and cruel blows; now subject to gibes and scorn
> and torturing tricks, now abandoned to the most
> loathsome necessities, or subject to the vilest and
> most outrageous violations. These are strong
> terms, but language fails to convey the astonishing
> truth. I proceed to verify this assertion, commenc-
> ing with the State of Maine ..."

None of the thirty states escaped Dix's scrutiny.
One by one she described what she had found. In
Georgia, she described what she had seen:

> "It was an intensely hot day when I visited F. He
> was confined in a roofed pen ... In warm weather,
> this wretched place was cleansed out once a week
> or fortnight; not so in the colder seasons. 'We have
> men called,' said his sister, 'and they go in and tie

him with ropes and throw him on the ground and throw water on him, and my husband cleans out the place.' But the expedient to prevent his freezing in winter was the most strangely horrible. In the centre of the pen was excavated a pit, six feet square, and deep; the top was closed over securely: and into this ghastly place, entered through a trap-door, was cast the maniac, there to exist till the returning warm weather induced his care-taker to withdraw him; there, without heat, without light, without pure air, was left the pining, miserable maniac, whose piteous groans and frantic cries might move to pity the hardest heart . . .

Her memorial concluded thus:

I ask relief for the East and for the West, for the North, and for the South . . . I ask for the people that which is already the property of the people . . . I ask for the thirty States of the Union, 5,000,000 acres of land, of the many hundreds of millions of public lands, appropriated in such a manner as shall assure the greatest benefits to all who are in circumstances of extreme necessity, and who, through the providence of God, are *wards of the nations*, claimants on the sympathy and care of the public, through the miseries and disqualifications brought upon them by the sorest afflictions with which humanity can be visited.

Respectfully submitted,
D.L.D.
Washington, June 23, 1848

Day after day, Dorothea Dix met with legislators in a special alcove in the Capitol Library, which Congress had voted to set aside for her. Despite the summer heat in Washington, Dorothea Dix faithfully maintained her daily schedule. Up at 4:15 a.m, she dressed, read her Bible, and meditated; from about 5:30 a.m. until 8:30 a.m. she wrote letters and articles; then she went to the dining room for breakfast and, after eating, she knitted while someone read the morning newspaper out loud; from 10:00 a.m. until 3:00 p.m she met with people in her alcove; returning home she read the paper or wrote until 4:30 p.m., when she had dinner; she sat with the family until 6:00 p.m., then went to her room and wrote until 8:00 p.m., when she returned to the parlor for tea. After that she either went to bed or wrote for an hour or two.

In January, she wrote to her brother Joseph, "... I am watching and guarding the 5,000,000 bill ... I am neither sanguine nor discouraged. I think the bill may be deferred till next session." She was right—her bill was deferred. Congress adjourned having never voted on D.L.D.'s bill. "There will be another session," Dorothea Dix wrote.

When Congress returned in December 1849, Dix was ready. This time she asked for 12,250,000 acres. A tidal wave of letters supporting her bill flooded Congress. Newspaper editorials, sermons, and resolutions from various organizations urged senators and representatives to pass her bill. Summer in Washington was unbearably hot that year, but Dix didn't slack off. Once again, however, Congress failed to pass her bill. "Dear Annie—My bill has been deferred to the first month of the next session," she wrote. "Pray that my patience may not fail utterly. I go to Maryland on Tuesday and directly to the interior of Pennsylvania."

Dorothea Dix was at her walnut desk in the alcove when Congress met again. By February 1851, the Senate was ready to vote. "My dear Friend:" she wrote to Anne while she waited, "My bill is up in the Senate. I am awaiting the result with great anxiety, but with a calmness which astonishes myself...

"Mr. Mason of Virginia sends me word the bill will pass—

"Mr. Shields just comes to say the bill will pass.—
You do not know how terrible this suspense!—I am
perfectly calm, and as cold as ice.

"4 p.m. The bill passed the Senate beautifully. A
large majority, more than two to one! ..."

Now, if only the House of Representatives would
pass the bill. But the House deferred it. And since the
bill had to pass *both* the Senate and the House in the
same session, Dix's land bill had failed once again.

Dorothea Dix was back in 1852. This time, in addition to 12,225,000 acres, she asked for $100,000 for
a hospital in Washington D.C., which would be for military people with mental illnesses. In August Congress
appropriated the $100,000 (and built what today is
called St. Elizabeths). As for her land bill, this time the
House of Representatives passed it and the Senate deferred it.

Finally, on March 9, 1854, Dorothea Dix's bill
passed the Senate by a large majority. Several days
later it was passed by the House of Representatives.
Success at last! After six long years, Dorothea Dix had
achieved a tremendous moral victory. Congress had
agreed to provide for people, who, "through the Providence of God, are wards of the nation." Now all that
was needed was President Franklin Pierce's signature.
Swamped with congratulations, Dorothea Dix hardly
had time to celebrate before she heard a terrible ru-
mor—Pierce was thinking about vetoing her land bill.
No! Dorothea Dix thought. Pierce had told her he favored
her idea. Weeks dragged by as Dix and her supporters
tried to line up enough votes to override Pierce's veto,
if indeed, he did such an unthinkable thing.

"Dear Annie—Poor weak man!" Dorothea Dix wrote
as she waited. Finally, in May, Franklin Pierce made up
his mind. He vetoed Dorothea Dix's bill. If Congress provided for the indigent insane people, he wrote in his veto

81

message, it would have to provide for "all the poor in all the states," whether they were insane or not. And for that reason he vetoed the bill — the responsibility for poor people belonged to the states, not the federal government.

Despite an intense effort, Dix and her supporters couldn't get enough votes to override Pierce's veto. The land grant bill was dead.

Dorothea Lynde Dix was devastated.

Here Dorothea Lynde Dix is at her desk in Washington in the 1850s, holding a memorial that she has written. (Photo courtesy of National Portrait Gallery, Smithsonian Institution.)

Chapter Ten

INDOMITABLE WOMAN: 1848-1854

Dorothea Dix was also exhausted. During the six years she had been lobbying Congress, she had traveled extensively, including Mississippi, Maryland, Nova Scotia, Alabama, and Florida. In 1848, after Congress deferred her land grant bill for the first time, she went to North Carolina. Traveling for three months, she investigated thirty-nine jails and almshouses. "I come not to urge personal claims," she wrote in her Memorial to the General Assembly of North Carolina. "I am the Hope of the poor crazed beings who pine in the cells, and stalls, and cages, and waste rooms of your poorhouses. I am the Revelation of hundreds of wailing, suffering creatures, hidden in your private dwellings, and in pens and cabins—shut out, cut off from all healing influences, from all mind-restoring cures."

A bill was presented to the General Assembly asking for $100,000 for a hospital for the insane. It was defeated. Shortly after its defeat, the bill was reintroduced by James C. Dobbin, a prominent legislator. Why did James Dobbin reintroduce the bill? Dorothea Dix had met Dobbin and his wife Louisa, who, like Dix, were staying at the Mansion House, a hotel in Raleigh, North Carolina, where the legislature was meeting.

During their stay, Louisa Dobbin became very ill. Dorothea Dix nursed her night and day. One night, Mrs. Dobbin gasped, "I fear I am sinking rapidly." Dix called the doctor and her husband. "You have been so kind to me—a stranger," Louisa Dobbin weakly whispered. "I wish to ask my husband to do something for you. What shall I ask him?" Without hesitation, Dorothea Dix replied, "Tell him to sponsor my hospital bill."

Louisa Dobbin died just before the vote, and Dorothea Dix accompanied James Dobbin with his wife's body to Fayetteville. Upon hearing that the bill had been defeated, Dix and Dobbin returned to Raleigh. Wearing a black band around his arm, as was the custom for people who were in mourning, Dobbin reintroduced the bill and proposed two new taxes—one cent on every $100 worth of land and two and one-half cents on every poll for four years—to pay for the hospital. Motivated by his promise to his wife and gratitude to Dorothea Dix, Dobbin gave a powerful speech that won the day. "Rejoice, rejoice with me!" Dorothea Dix wrote Harriet Hare. "Through toil, anxiety, and tribulation, my bill has passed! 101 ayes, 10 nayes. I am not well, though perfectly happy. I leave North Carolina compensated a thousand-fold for all labors by this great success."

Alabama was next. Dorothea Dix traveled five straight days and nights, with only one stop long enough to bathe. Just before the vote, the state capitol burned down, and the legislature adjourned without passing the hospital bill. "Dear Annie ... I have passed amidst dark and rough ways before and shall not now give out," Dorothea Dix wrote. Happily, two years later, the Alabama legislature voted to build a hospital.

While she was in Alabama, Dorothea Dix wrote her Memorial to the Honorable Legislative Assembly of the Province of Nova Scotia and its Dependencies. In 1844 and 1848 Dix had toured Nova Scotia, which is almost completely surrounded by the Atlantic Ocean and connected to the mainland of Canada only by a small isthmus.

> "Gentlemen: Your memorialist respectfully asks attention in your legislative capacity to a subject embracing the welfare of a numerous and fast-increasing class of your fellow-citizens ... I refer to the insane of all classes and ages, and of both sexes, numbered now by hundreds ..."

As were all her memorials, Dix's Nova Scotia memorial was thoroughly researched, carefully thought out, and eloquently written. Aware, after her years of experience, that many politicians and taxpayers were more concerned with their wallets than their hearts, Dix included "A Table Showing the Comparative Cost to the State of Twenty Old and Twenty Recent Cases of Insanity, Illustrating the Importance in An Economical Point of View of Placing Such Persons Under Treatment at an Early Period of Their Disease, and of Providing Every Means of Treating Them Successfully in an Asylum." According to Dix's figures in the table, it was cheaper to build hospitals in which people got cured than to pay to keep them in jails and almshouses where they didn't.

After appealing to their pocketbooks, D.L. Dix urged the legislators to:

> "In imagination, ... enter the horrid, noisome cell, invest yourselves with the foul, tattered garments which scantily serve the purposes of decent protection; cast yourselves upon the loathsome pile of filthy straw; find companionship in your own cries and groans, or in the wailings and gibberings of wretches miserable like yourselves; call for help and release, for blessed words of soothing and kind offices of care, till the dull walls are weary in

sending back the echo of your moans; then, if self-possession is not overwhelmed under the imaginary miseries of what are the actually distresses of the insane, return to the consciousness of your sound intellectual health, and answer if you will longer refuse or delay to make adequate appropriations for the establishment of a provincial hospital ... Shall Nova Scotia be last and least in responding to the loud calls of humanity ... Your memorialist believes otherwise, and in the confidence this belief inspires respectfully submits this cause to the Honorable Assembly of which she addresses this appeal.

D.L. Dix
From Montgomery, Alabama, and forwarded to Halifax from Washington, D.C., United States of America, December 10, A.D. 1849."

While her memorial was being presented and a hospital bill was being passed in Nova Scotia, Dorothea Dix was in Mississippi. In February 1850 her Memorial Soliciting Adequate Appropriations for the Construction of a State Hospital for the Insane in the State of Mississippi was presented.

"Twenty-four majority in the Senate and eighty-one in the House, was something of a conquest over prejudice and the positive declaration and determination not to give a dime!" she wrote in triumph to Harriet Hare. In addition to appropriating $50,000, the Mississippi legislature voted to provide 3,000,000 bricks for the new hospital and to rebuild the state penitentiary.

During her stay in Mississippi, Dorothea Dix also added to her collection of travel adventures.

"We have on our boat," she wrote to Harriet Hare, "both cholera and malignant scarlet fever. To add to our various incidents, a quantity of gunpowder was left in charge of a raw Irishman, who was directed, at a given time and place, to load the cannon and fire a salute. One hundred miles away from the point to be so honored, Pat, thinking the bore of the cannon as good a place of deposit for the powder as he could find, rammed it down. Then, discovering that the rain had wet the bore, he ran with alacrity to the furnace and returned with a burning stick, thrusting it in after the powder, 'to dry up the wather.' This it effected, but not this alone, for of course the powder exploded, and certain portions of Pat's arm and hand were sent in advance toward the distant city."

Dorothea Dix, of course, tended to poor Pat's injuries.

The miles added up—close to 80,000 by now—as Dorothea Dix continued her crusade into Maryland, Florida, and South Carolina. Fredricka Bremer, a famous novelist from Sweden who visited America, accompanied Dorothea Dix on several trips. "She is one of the most beautiful proofs of that which a woman, without any other aid than her own free will and character, without any other power than that of her purpose and its uprightness, and her ability to bring these forward, can effect in society ...," Bremer wrote. She was astonished at Dix's drive and fortitude.

Nothing fazed Dorothea Dix—not drinking muddy river water, cockroaches in her luggage, or mice running freely around her cabin. In one cabin where the cockroaches and mice were particularly bad, Bremer recalled later, Dorothea Dix calmly got out of bed, lit a candle, and moved their baggage to a safer place. At every stop along the way, Dix was the first one down the gangplank and the last one to board before the boat left again. She never missed an opportunity to check out the local jail or almshouse.

To conserve her energy, Dorothea Dix kept her life simple. On long trips, she sent one small trunk ahead, but most of the time, she traveled with a medium-sized valise. Her clothes never varied — plain gray dresses with white collars and cuffs for traveling and simple, but striking, black or dark colored dresses for special occasions. Anne Heath and her sister Abby sewed her dresses when she wore them out. Her luggage was more likely to be bulging with books, gifts, and specimens of new plants, for which she was always on the lookout, than with clothes.

In 1853, the year before Pierce vetoed her hospital bill, Dix traveled to St. John's on Newfoundland, a large island above Nova Scotia and off the northeastern coast of Canada. A ferocious storm hit while she was there. For days, the ocean roared. Dorothea Dix heard talk that Sable Island had been devastated. Sable Island, Dix found out, was four hundred miles out in the ocean south of Newfoundland. At one time a convict colony, Sable Island was the scene of many shipwrecks. The bones of many sailors littered the island. Desolate and dangerous, Sable Island had one relief station with a life-saving crew. What kind of equipment did they have, Dorothea Dix asked? Was it up-to-date? Were there enough boats? Unable to get enough answers to satisfy her, Dix decided to go to Sable Island herself. It was a dangerous trip, Hugh Bell, the mayor of Halifax, warned her. Dix listened politely and boarded the next boat to Sable Island.

Hiring a little native pony, Dorothea Dix rode around the island for several days, surveying the remains of wrecked ships, talking with the live-saving crew, and inspecting their equipment. Clearly it was inadequate. During her visit, a ship wrecked. Dix watched the rescue. All the ship's crew was saved except the captain who refused to be rescued. He's a raving lunatic, the life-savers told Dorothea Dix. Return and save him, she insisted. But he's mad, the life-savers repeated. Again Dorothea Dix insisted they return. Finally the life-savers brought the captain ashore bound hand and foot. Dorothea Dix untied the ropes and took him by the arm. She stayed with the captain and talked in a soothing voice until he regained his senses. Let him rest and give him nourishing food and he will be fine, Dorothea Dix instructed the crew.

Upon her return to Boston, Dorothea Dix set about securing adequate life-saving equipment for Sable Island. Contacting Captain Robert W. Forbes, an expert on life-saving equipment, she sought his opinion about the proper equipment. "Trying experiments with life-preservers and boats. I went into the river with a neighbor to show Miss Dix how to capsize and how to right a boat. We invited her to throw herself over and permit us to save her, but, as she had no change of clothes, she declined," Forbes wrote in his journal.

Within months, Dorothea Dix had raised enough money to have four lifeboats built. Listening to Forbes' warning not to send all the boats together, Dix arranged for one boat, *Victoria*, to be sent on a steamer. The other three boats, which Dix named *Grace Darling*, *The Reliance*, and *The Samaritan*, were sent on the brig *Eleanora*, along with two boat wagons, one life car, the mortar with ammunition, coils of manila rope, and other accessories. Dix had already sent a large library of books. Unfortunately Forbes' warning was justified. *Eleanora* ran ashore and the lifeboats were severely damaged. Undaunted, Dix arranged to have the lifeboats brought back to New York City for repairs. Less than a year later, all the equipment arrived safely on Sable Island. Now, in addition to hospitals, penitentiaries, almshouses, and orphanages, Dorothea Dix visited life-saving stations along the Atlantic coast. Along with proper equipment, Dix made sure the life-savers had plenty of books and magazines.

By the time the equipment arrived at Sable Island, Pierce had vetoed Dix's bill, and she plunged into deep despair. Her grand plan had failed. Of course, there was an enormous amount of other work to do; hospitals and penitentiaries to visit; problems to solve. Each day, bundles of mail arrived full of requests from doctors, superintendents, wardens, politicians, and citizens throughout the land. But Dorothea Dix had lost her drive. Exhausted and depressed, she knew that she needed to get away. To leave the disappointment behind. To try to restore herself. Once before Dorothea Dix had regained her strength in England, at the Rathbones' home, Greenbank.

Would it work again?

Chapter Eleven

THE AMERICAN INVADER: 1854-1856

On September 2, 1854, Dorothea Dix boarded the steamship *Arctic* bound for England. E.K. Collins, owner of the steamship company, refused to let her pay for her ticket. Such gestures weren't unusual. Years earlier, John Adams Dix (no relation to Dorothea), President of the Chicago and Rock Island Railroad, had sent her a free pass, as had the owners of other railroad and steamboat companies. Since 1848, the Adams and Company Express Office had been shipping all of her packages free — a huge savings considering the hundreds of books and supplies Dorothea Dix was continually sending to hospitals and prisons. Dix never asked for or expected such favors. But she always accepted them and used the money she saved to advance her cause. In this case she bought a life insurance policy to benefit the New Jersey State Lunatic Asylum.

> "Dear Annie—Thus far, by the good providence of God," she related in a letter written after nine days at sea, "we are safely on our voyage. I am now free from seasickness. I pass the time with such measure of listlessness as affords but few results that will tell for others' good. However, I give you an example of my success. I had observed on Sunday

WRECK OF THE U.S.M. STEAM SHIP "ARCTIC"

Dorothea Dix traveled to England on the U.S.M. steamship Arctic *in September 1854. The* Arctic *sank on its return trip to New York. (Photo courtesy of The Mariners' Museum, Newport News, Virginia.)*

several parties betting on the steamer's run. I waited till the bets were decided, and then asked the winner for the winnings, which I put in the Captain's care for 'The Home for the Children of Indigent Sailors' in New York. Tonight I am going to ask each passenger for a donation for the same object as our thank offering for preservation thus far on our voyage. I shall, I think, get above $150, or perhaps but $100."

Dorothea Dix's idea of a thank offering for a safe voyage took on special meaning when, after Dix was in England, the news came that on its return trip, *Arctic* had sunk.

The Rathbones met Dix in Liverpool and took her

to Greenbank. The estate and gardens were as beautiful as she had remembered, and the Rathbones as caring and loving. As always, the Rathbones' house was alive with stimulating conversation. Leading reformers, important scientists, and outstanding writers and thinkers had been coming to the Rathbones' estate for years. Hearing that Dorothea Dix, whose reputation was well-known in Europe, was there, they came in increasing numbers to meet with her. It was an exhilarating but exhausting time. "Dear Annie—I am still here with dear friends," she wrote, "much occupied with charitable institutions and the meetings of the British Scientific Association. All this tires me sadly, but I shall take things easier in a week."

Her idea of taking things easier was to spend four weeks touring Ireland. Naturally, she inspected almost every hospital, asylum, and workhouse, all of which she found acceptable. She also found time to enjoy herself. In a letter to Mrs. Rathbone, she described her visit to a castle where Lord Ross invited her to look through his telescope. There she was, Dix wrote, "swinging in mid-air, sixty feet from the ground at two in the morning ... on a massive gallery, looking through the most magnificent telescope in the world."

Returning to Greenbank, she found a letter from Hugh Bell in Newfoundland.

"Dear Madam, The very day after the arrival of the largest lifeboat [*The Reliance*] at Sable Island, ... a large American ship from Antwerp with upwards of one hundred and sixty passengers, men, women, and children, was cast upon one of the sandbanks off the northeast end of the island, and lurched so that the sea beat into her and rendered all chance of escape by the efforts of the people on board quite hopeless. The sea was so heavy, and the weather so boisterous, that none of the island's boats could live in it ... Your *Reliance* rode over the waves, as

93

the sailors said, like a duck, and with her and two of your smaller boats, the *Samaritan* and the *Rescue*, the whole of the passengers were safely landed; poor things, almost in a state of nudity..."

News of the dramatic rescue and the role of Dix's lifeboats spread rapidly. She received many letters of appreciation, including one from a mother whose son had been rescued. Typically, Dix insisted that the life-saving crew deserved all the credit, and she arranged for them to receive medals for their bravery from the Royal Humane Society.

By and large, Dorothea Dix discovered that mentally ill people received decent care in England. Members of the "Society for Improving the Condition of the Insane" worked hard to make life better for mentally ill people. Conditions in Scotland, Dorothea Dix heard, were a different story. Arriving in Edinburgh, the capital of Scotland, in February 1855, she wrote to Anne Heath, "Dear Annie,—... It is true I came here for plea-sure [referring to the original reason for her trip to England], but that is no reason why I should close my eyes to the condition of these most helpless of God's creatures."

Some of the institutions she visited were "good, very good," others, however, were terrible. Dix was de-termined to do something. But what? Nothing, some people told her, because she was a foreigner — an "American Invader," in the words of one political leader. Other people, like the Rathbones, worried about her health.

"I am not so very ill," Dorothea Dix replied to Mrs. Rathbone, "... I am not *naturally* very active, and *never do* anything there is a fair chance *other* people will take up. So, when you know I am busy, you may be sure it is leading the forlorn hope,—which I conduct to a successful termination through a certain sort of

94

obstinacy that some people make the blunder of calling zeal, and the yet greater blunder of having its first inciting cause in philanthropy. I have no particular love for my species at large, but own to an exhaustless fund of compassion."

Having nursed Dorothea Dix back to health after her complete physical and emotional breakdown, Mrs. Rathbone undoubtedly understood the source of Dix's "exhaustless fund of compassion." Dorothea Dix had been there. She had been an invalid in both her mind and body. And not just once, but twice. Yet under the care of kind people in pleasant surroundings, first with the Channings in St. Croix and then with the Rathbones at Greenbank, she had recovered. Dorothea Dix's compassion grew out of her own experience. Perhaps also, although she would never talk about it, her experience of growing up with an invalid mother and unstable father had greatly affected her.

Now Dorothea Dix's compassion was directed toward mentally ill people in Scotland. After consulting with sympathetic people in Scotland, Dix decided that the best solution was to get an official Commission for Investigation established. Because Scotland was under the laws of England, such a Commission could only be established by the Home Secretary, Sir George Grey, whose office was located in London. Concerned that officials in Edinburgh, who wanted to undermine her report, might get to Grey first, Dorothea Dix decided to waste no time in leaving for London.

> "I looked into my purse," she later wrote in a long letter to her friend, Mrs. Samuel Torrey, in Boston, "and counted time, and considered my health,—for I had not felt so strong for some days as I could desire,—but my conscience told me quite distinctly what was my duty. I took, then, my carpet-bag, and wrapping about me my warm traveling garments, called a cab, and at a quarter past nine p.m. put

myself into the express train direct for London, expecting to arrive in twelve hours, four hundred miles. I first telegraphed to Lord Shaftesbury [the person who could arrange for Dix to meet with Sir George], asking an interview at three p.m. the following day, and naming the King's Cross Station as my point of arrival. I did not sleep, but was comfortable. An accident at nine a.m. detained the train till eleven a.m., which should have arrived an hour and a half earlier.

"I had never been in London, knew *not one location*, I stepped from the royal mail carriage, and a gentlemen in a moment asked if I was Miss Dix, and announced a messenger from Lord Shaftesbury, accepting my appointment . . .

"I looked at my watch. It was only an hour to twelve. I had not time to dress for presentation, took a cab, . . . threw off my traveling cloak in the cab for a velvet I had in my hand, folded a cashmere shawl on, and believe I did not look so much amiss as one traveling so far might look . . ."

Dorothea Dix persuaded Sir George to appoint the commission. Within two years, the commission substantiated Dix's findings and reforms were underway in Scotland.

Worn out by her efforts, Dorothea Dix accepted Dr. Hack Tuke's invitation to recuperate at York Retreat, one of the first places to provide moral treatment for mentally ill people. The grandson of William Tuke, who had founded York Retreat, and son of Samuel, who had run it for years, Hack Tuke was a great admirer of Dorothea Dix, and, himself, an expert on moral treatment.

Dix welcomed the opportunity to study what was going on at York Retreat. But first she had to get well. "Counting the time since I left the steamer," she confided in a letter to Dr. Buttolph, superintendent of

Trenton Asylum and her personal physician, "I find that rather more than half the period I have been either really too ill or too languid to do anything. The irritation of the mucous membrane of the stomach has of late affected me more seriously, and the inaction of the heart has left me feeble."

As had happened so often before, when Dr. Tuke told her about the bad conditions on the Channel Islands, Jersey and Guernsey, off the coast of England, Dorothea Dix rallied to overcome her illness. "There, my friend, this must help me get well soon!" she wrote in a letter to Dr. Buttolph in which she described the situation in the Channel Islands.

Arriving on Jersey in July 1855, Dix found mentally ill people in a "... horrid state, naked, filthy ..." Before long she persuaded the governing body to build a new hospital. Again, congratulations poured in. Mrs. E.H. Walsh, wife of the American ambassador to France wrote to a friend in England, "Pray remember me to Miss Dix. If with you, tell her that I kiss the hem of her garment, and bless God that our country has produced such a noble heart. She will see the honorable mention of her services by the Earl of Shaftesbury in Parliament, and Mr. Walsh is about to add his testimony to her immense worth, in his correspondence. He regrets very much not having made the acquaintance of Miss Dix. He is right. Such a woman is to be worshiped if anything human could be worshiped."

"Dear Annie — People here seem to think I have done a great work," she wrote, "Perhaps I have. I know it is certainly very satisfying and I feel right about it at heart, and a thousand times happier than if I had wasted my time doing nothing for the good of others."

The Rathbones urged Dorothea Dix to join them for a vacation in Switzerland. Reluctantly she agreed. But once there, she fell in love with the "... snow-clad

A letter Anne Heath wrote to Dorothea Dix while she was in Europe recovering from her disappointment after President Pierce vetoed her land bill. In the letter Anne Heath refers to Pierce as "that counterfeit President ... a New Hampshire traitor ..." In the second paragraph Heath writes, "Yr [your] note of Apr. [April] 28th was most anxiously waited for, & a great relief when it came—for I feared you might be made sick,—but the Evil eye must fall on a more faltering character to have any withering effect." She ends the letter with the words, "You are a tree planted by the waters & therefore safe. With heartfelt love & sympathy, Yrs. [Yours] A.E. Heath." (Reproduced by permission of the Houghton Library, Harvard University.)

98

peaks, mantled with their regal robes of pasture and forest ..." Here she was able to indulge herself in her passion for nature and science. Taking long carriage and horseback rides, she studied geological formations and glaciers and collected new specimens of plants. Years later Dorothea Dix wrote, "I never find the glorious view of the Alps fade from my mind's eye. A thousand incidents recall and repeat the memory of those grand snow peaks piercing the skies."

Thoroughly refreshed, Dorothea Dix set off on an extraordinary tour of hospitals, prisons, and asylums in Europe. Speaking no other language than English and a bit of French, she traveled alone for three months through France, Italy, Greece, Turkey, Austria-Hungary, Germany, Russia, and Scandinavia. "Dear Annie —" she wrote from a steamer in Hungary, "I find traveling here alone no more difficult than I should in any part of America. My usual experience attend me. People are civil and obliging, who are treated civilly ..."

When Dix discovered terrible conditions in a hospital in Rome, she went to see the Pope, who went to see for himself. Appalled by what he saw, he thanked Dix and set about getting a new hospital built. In Turkey, she reported to Mrs. Rathbone, "The insane of Constantinople [today called Istanbul] are in *far better condition* than those of Rome or Trieste ... The hospital was founded by Solyman the Magnificent, and the provisions for the comfort and pleasure of the patients, including music, quite astonished me. I had substantially little to suggest, and nothing to urge!" In Vienna she stayed longer than usual to discuss new ideas about mental illness, and to promote the plans for a new hospital. In Russia, she wrote, "I saw much to approve and appreciate ... As for the hospitals in St. Petersburg and Moscow ... Every comfort and all needed care were possessed, and much recreation secured.

Very little restraint was used."

Dorothea Dix had consulted with the leading experts on mental illness in Europe. She had seen all kinds of hospitals, asylums, and prisons. She had learned about the latest treatments. Everywhere she went, she left her mark — reforms were undertaken, new hospitals built, and new friends made. "Missed you so much after you left," one new friend wrote to her. "You would think it foolish, my dear Miss Dix, if I told you how much I loved you."

Well-known throughout Europe before her visit, now she was famous. Tributes and testimonies overwhelmed her. But it was time to leave. Every day the mail contained numerous appeals from America for her help. And her close friend Millard Fillmore was running for president. Finally, in September 1856, Dorothea Dix boarded a ship bound for America. She had been away for two years. What would she find when she returned, she wondered?

Chapter Twelve

DESPITE THE STORM: 1856-1861

America was in a crisis — a crisis that had been building for years. The issue was slavery. Was it going to be allowed to spread in the United States or wasn't it? Was it going to be allowed to exist at all?

The first black Africans were sold as slaves in America in 1619, more than 150 years before the start of the Revolutionary War. Arriving aboard a Dutch frigate, twenty people bound in chains were bought by settlers in Jamestown, Virginia, the first permanent English colony in North America. It wasn't long before hundreds of thousands of slaves—black men, women, and children from Africa — toiled long hours in tobacco, rice, indigo, and cotton fields. Although from the beginning some white Americans spoke out against slavery, it was legal in all thirteen colonies until 1777 when Vermont became the first state to abolish it. Gradually other northern states abolished slavery, but it continued to flourish in southern states.

Dorothea Dix was well aware of the horrors of slavery. The whips, manacles, leg irons, and slave auctions where, in the words of a former slave named Robinson, "The purchasers go around, make the slaves open their mouths, that they may look in, as they would a horse, feel of their limbs, strip them, & make them run, jump & try all their physical powers. In the cases of the girls, they often lift up their clothes & feel of their legs, feel their bosoms, & try all their feminine points ..."

She was also well aware of the abolitionists, or people determined to end slavery. Many of Dix's closest friends and supporters of her crusade—Julia Ward Howe, Samuel Gridley Howe, Horace Mann, George Emerson, Charles Sumner—were outspoken abolitionists. It was a topic that dominated their conversations. She also read *The Liberator*, the anti-slavery newspaper William Lloyd Garrison had been publishing in Boston since 1831, the year she started her secondary school. And she paid close attention to the actions of Congress. The first important act, the Missouri Compromise of 1820, temporarily settled the issue of slavery by admitting Missouri as a slave state and Maine as a free state, and by prohibiting the spread of slavery in land north of the southern boundary of Missouri. Fourteen years later, Congress repealed the Missouri Compromise by passing the Kansas-Nebraska Bill that allowed the people in each territory to decide whether or not to introduce slavery.

Passed by Congress on May 30, 1854 (seven days before Franklin Pierce vetoed Dix's 12,225,000 Acre Bill) the Kansas-Nebraska Act resulted in open warfare. Pro- and anti-slavery settlers fought for control. Anti-slavery settlers came from as far away as Massachusetts to establish the town of Lawrence, Kansas. Pro-slavery settlers came from neighboring Missouri and set Lawrence on fire. John Brown, with a small group of men, attacked a small settlement of pro-slavery settlers, murdering five of them. Violence reigned everywhere, even on the floor of Congress where Representative Preston S. Brooks of South Carolina attacked and almost killed Senator Charles Sumner of Massachusetts (a key supporter of Dix's first crusade in Massachusetts and her later one in Congress). "I gave him about thirty first-rate stripes. Towards the last, he bellowed like a calf," Brooks boasted to reporters later. "I wore my cane out completely but saved the head—which is gold."

The country was in turmoil over the issue of slavery, yet Dorothea Dix chose to remain silent. At least, in public she did. "These beings (slave owners), I repeat, *cannot* be *Christians*, they cannot act as moral beings, they cannot live as souls destined for immortality," she had written in a letter to Mrs. Samuel Torrey in 1831 after seeing slavery firsthand on St. Croix. "No blessing, no good, can follow in the path trodden by slavery."

Given Dix's strong moral feelings and outspoken nature, her public silence on the issue of slavery perplexed some of her friends. However, Dorothea Dix had always kept herself apart from all the other reform movements of her lifetime, including temperance, anti-capital punishment, peace, and the powerful movement for women's rights. In part, this was because of her style; Dorothea Dix worked within the existing political system, through state legislatures and the United States Congress. As Dix once told William Rathbone, she got things done "By going to people whose duty it is to set things right, assuming that they will do so without disturbance being made, and they generally do so." She didn't see the need to form outside organizations. And there were so many—the American Society for the Collection and Diffusion of Information on Punishment by Death or The Friends of Universal Reform or The American Peace Society. Dorothea Dix avoided all of them. Nor did she think it was necessary to add her voice to causes like the women's rights movement, which already had such strong leaders as Lucretia Mott, Elizabeth Cady Stanton, and Susan B. Anthony.

But more important, Dorothea Dix was determined not to let anything distract her from her own crusade, or to let her beliefs and behavior become issues that could hurt her cause. Even the rumors that she was an abolitionist were enough to help defeat her hospital bill the first time it was introduced in North Carolina. She wasn't going to risk her work by taking sides on the issue of slavery, especially with so much of her work going on in the South. And there was so much to do. Dorothea Dix was as busy as she ever had been.

"Dear Annie — Tues I spent at Ward's, Randall's, and Blackwell's Island," she wrote on December 26, 1856 from New York City. "Wednesday up the Hudson (River) to Sing Sing prison, on Thursday (today) High Bridge, to juvenile asylums, and reformatories; tomorrow to Bloomingdales; Saturday, hospitals in the city, and Saturday evening to Trenton. Thus you see the progress of my doings. I now think I shall go to Philadelphia on Tuesday, on Wednesday make the purchases for the hospital at Harrisburg, on Thursday go to Harrisburg, a day's journey, see the patients Friday; return to Philadelphia Saturday, spend Sunday at the hospital; Monday, almshouses; Tuesday Trenton; Wednesday set out for Buffalo, Geneva, Canandaigua, etc., to explain anew the miseries of their almshouses, so if you do not hear from me, please do not consider yourself forgotten or even unbeloved."

The scope of her activities was widespread: visiting patients, inspecting institutions, buying supplies, raising money, writing reports, and soliciting donations of books, pictures, billiard tables, pianos, and marble statues. And giving advice. She was constantly being asked for advice — about the best site for a hospital, the best design, the best superintendent to run it, and the

Dorothea Dix was always donating items to benefit patients, such as this elegant stagecoach. After raising the money, Dix had the coach built by Hall & Bartlett of Rockford, Illinois, and then shipped to the Illinois Hospital for the Insane. It seated eleven people. (Photo courtesy of Harvard College Library.)

best way to treat patients.

In addition, she was frequently asked to resolve such disputes as complaints from patients about their treatment, disagreements between superintendents and other staff members, and complaints from politicians about how much money was being spent. Sometimes, disgruntled people would criticize Dorothea Dix's decisions. But that didn't bother her. "My dear Annie," she wrote after an incident in Worcester, "do not take too much to heart that which people say in Worcester, it is as the weight of a feather to me. I am *right*, what harm can these do me?"

These were enormously productive years for Dorothea Dix. Hospitals were being built and expanded, prisons improved and reformed, and mental illness continued to lose its stigma. In addition, progress was being made toward implementing another one of Dix's goals — training programs for nurses and attendants who worked in mental hospitals.

Although her friends always worried about her stamina and frequently admonished her to rest, Dix continued to travel throughout the country.

"Dear Annie—I do not know whether you have followed my devious journey," Dorothea Dix wrote from Nashville, Tennessee in July 1858, "but if you will look on the map for Philadelphia, Baltimore, Washington, Chesapeake Bay, Norfolk, Williamsburg, York, Hampton, Portsmouth, Raleigh, North Carolina, Weldon, Petersburg, Richmond, Charlottesville, Trenton, Rockbridge, Central Virginia, Salem, Abington [sic], Bristol, Virginia, Dalton, Georgia, Chattanooga and Nashville you will follow my devious course."

In the spring of 1859, Dorothea Dix left for Texas, a sparsely settled, rugged land in those days. Her friends were horrified. Texas was too primitive for a woman traveling alone, they said. Nonsense, Dorothea Dix said.

Travel was difficult in Texas, and the living conditions were hard, but Dorothea Dix was amazed at the reception she received. "I am thankful I have come," she wrote to Mrs. Hare from Austin, Texas, "because I find much to do, and people take me by the hand as a beloved friend." In another letter she wrote to Mrs. Torrey:

"I was taking dinner at a small public house on a wide, lonely prairie. The master stood, with the stage way-bill in his hands, reading and eyeing me, I thought, because I was the only lady passenger, but, when I drew out my purse to pay as usual, his quick expression was, 'No, no, by George! I don't take money from you; why, I never thought I should see you, and now you are in my house! You have done

106

good to everybody for years and years. Make sure now there's a home for you in every house in Texas. Here, wife, this is Miss Dix! Shake hands, and call the children.'

"Don't think me conceited in relating this incident," she added.

With the election of Abraham Lincoln as president in November 1860, it was clear that the country was going to explode. "I thank God, dear Annie," Dorothea wrote in February 1861, "I have such full uses for time now, for the state of our beloved country, otherwise, would crush my heart and life. I was never so unhappy but once before and that grief was more selfish perhaps, when the 12,225 Acre Bill was killed by a poor, base man in power."

In March, just before Lincoln's inauguration, she wrote, "Dear Annie, All my Bills have passed. My winter has been fully successful. I have had great cares, great fatigues, many dangers, countless blessings, unmeasured, preserving mercies, and am joined to all occasion for thanksgiving—well, and still able to work very satisfactorily—God spare our distressed country!"

Because she traveled extensively throughout the South, Dorothea Dix knew better than most Northerners how dire the situation was. Everywhere she went she heard talk of war. On one trip, she learned about a well-organized plot to prevent Lincoln from being inaugurated as President of the United States. Arranging a private meeting with Samuel M. Felton, President of the Philadelphia and Baltimore Railroad and the man responsible for transporting Lincoln from his home in Illinois to Washington, D.C., Dorothea Dix told him about the plan.

"I listened for more than an hour," Felton wrote in an account of their crucial meeting. "The sum of it

107

was that there was an extensive and organized conspiracy through the South to seize Washington ... then declare the Southern Confederacy de facto Government of the United States. At the same time, they were to cut off all means of communication between Washington and the North, East, and West, and thus prevent the transportation of troops ... Mr. Lincoln's inauguration was thus to be prevented, or his life was to fall a sacrifice. In fact, she said, troops were then drilling on the line of our own road ..."

Convinced of the danger, Felton hired detectives, who managed to join the troops and confirm Dix's account. Felton then devised a plan to smuggle Lincoln into the Capital. For years after the incident, Felton tried to get Dorothea Dix's permission to "make known how much the country owed to her, but that she had always given a point-blank refusal to have any use made of her name." (A consequence of Dix's refusal is that most historians give the credit to Allan Pinkerton, a detective.)

About six weeks after Lincoln's inauguration, on April 12, 1861, the first shots of the Civil War were fired at Fort Sumter. Three days later, President Abraham Lincoln called for 75,000 volunteers. Within a week, thousands of northern troops were pouring into Washington. Dorothea Dix, who had been resting in Trenton after her strenuous trip west, came with them. She, too, wanted to serve her country. Thus at the age of fifty-nine, Dorothea Lynde Dix undertook a new challenge. A challenge about which she eventually said, "This is not the work I would have my life judged by!"

Chapter Thirteen

DOING HER DUTY: 1861-1867

"Dear Annie," Dorothea Dix wrote from Washington during the week when thousands of soldiers poured into the city in response to Lincoln's request, "It was not easy getting across the city, but I did not choose to turn back, and so I reached my place of destination. I think my duty lies near military hospitals for the present ... I have reported myself and some nurses for free service at the War Department and to the Surgeon General."

Secretary of War Cameron, gladly accepting Dorothea Dix's offer, issued an order:

"Be it known to all whom it may concern that the free services of Miss D.L. Dix are accepted by the War Department; and that she will give, at all times, all necessary aid in organizing Military Hospitals, for the care of all the sick or wounded soldiers; aiding the Chief Surgeon by supplying nurses and substantial means for the comfort and relief of the suffering; also, that she is fully authorized to receive, control and disburse special supplies bestowed by individuals or associations for the comfort of their friends or the citizen soldiers from all parts of the United States, as also under sanction of the Acting Surgeon General, to draw from the Army stores."

Seven weeks later, Dix was commissioned Superintendent of the Female Nurses of the Army, the first one in American history. As such, Dorothea Lynde Dix was given more authority and power than any other woman had had in the military prior to and during the Civil War.

Strange as it may seem to modern readers, at the time of the Civil War, nursing was not considered a proper profession for women—women were considered too emotional, too weak, and too squeamish for the job. Nursing was a man's job; at least, nursing that took place outside the home was a man's job. In fact, when the Civil War began there were no trained women nurses in the country.

Slowly, attitudes about women as nurses were changing. During the 1840s when Dorothea Dix was reforming the care of mentally ill people, Florence Nightingale, an Englishwoman, was learning everything she could about effective nursing methods. In 1854, the year of Pierce's veto and Dix's departure for England, the British government asked Nightingale to care for the thousands of British soldiers wounded during the Crimean War, a war Britain fought with Turkey and France against Russia (and the first war reported on by war correspondents and photographers). When Dorothea Dix was in Turkey, she visited the military hospital in Scutari that Nightingale had transformed from a foul, chaotic institution into a model of cleanliness and orderliness. Although Dix was disappointed that Florence Nightingale was away so she couldn't talk with her, Dix was impressed with the nursing methods she saw being practiced.

Now, five years later, Dorothea Dix was responsible for organizing Union nurses to serve in another war.

A war in which, before it ended, almost two million Union soldiers fought in over 2,400 battles. Some 300,000 Northern men died and another 400,000 were wounded.

Dorothea Dix served for the duration of the war— four years during which she comforted countless numbers of wounded and dying soldiers, and during which she infuriated and alienated many surgeons, officers, and volunteers. "Miss Dix has plagued us a little," wrote George Templeton Strong, a member of the United Sanitary Commission, a private relief agency. "She is energetic, benevolent, unselfish, and a mild case of monomania. Working on her own hook, she does good, but no one can cooperate with her, for she belongs to the class of comets and can be subdued into relations with no system whatever."

The tasks facing Dorothea Dix were staggering, as were the obstacles. The Army's Medical Department had fewer than 100 surgeons and the largest hospital, located in Kansas and far from the battlefields, had forty beds. Her ideas about cleanliness, proper diet, and good ventilation, which she had implemented in mental hospitals, were not widely accepted by military people. And her high moral standards and insistence of total dedication to the care of patients were beyond the reach of most people. Time and time again, Dorothea Dix lambasted surgeons who drank on duty (a common occurrence) and nurses who weren't "ready for duty at any hour of day or night." As her old friend Dr. Samuel Gridley Howe described her, "Miss Dix, who is the terror of all mere formalists, idlers, and evil-doers, goes there [a Washington hospital], as she goes everywhere, to prevent and remedy abuses and shortcomings." It wasn't long before surgeons and hospital administrators were complaining to the Surgeon General about her "prying and poking about."

Plunging into her work, Dorothea Dix helped set up hospitals, all marked by a yellow flag, in churches, hotels, schools, a silk factory, railroad stations, and a coach factory. Renting a house on H Street (later a bigger one on the corner of 14th Street and New York Avenue), she took charge of hospital supplies—receiving them, storing them, and distributing them to various hospitals. She also ordered supplies—500 long cotton hospital shirts made by women in Boston, socks knitted by women in Philadelphia, bandages rolled by women in Chicago, jellies and canned goods sent from New York, and bushels of lint (used for packing wounds and made by unraveling coarse material or scraping it with a sharp knife blade).

She also processed thousands of applications from women who wanted to be nurses. (By the end of the war, almost 3,200 women served as Union nurses. They received $12.50 a month while male nurses received $20.50 a month.) As with everything, Dorothea Dix had strong ideas about who should and shouldn't be nurses. She issued a circular, which was approved by the Surgeon General, listing her requirements:

> "No candidate for service in the Women's Department for nursing in the Military Hospitals of the United States, will be received below the age of thirty-five years, nor above fifty.
>
> "Only women of strong health, not subject of chronic disease, nor liable to sudden illnesses, need apply. The duties of the station make large and continued demands on strength.
>
> "Matronly persons of experience, good conduct, or superior education and serious disposition, will always have preference; habits of neatness, order, sobriety, and industry, are prerequisites ...
>
> "Dress plain, (colors brown, grey, or black) and

while connected with the service without ornaments of any sort.

"No applicants accepted for less than three months' service; those for longer periods always have preference."

D.L. Dix.
Approved. William A. Hammond, Surgeon General

Dix's directive was very unpopular. "Are we to be surrounded by ugly crones who can't wear even an earbob or a breast pin?" one surgeon wrote to another. And a woman who Dix had rejected complained, "Dragon Dix ... won't accept the services of any *pretty* nurses." Her directive was also unrealistic; in particular, the age restriction. Several women, who became famous nurses, went around Dix and reported directly to the battlefield; women such as Clara Barton, who was too young for Dix, and Mary Ann Bickerdyke, who was too old. Before long, as maimed and dying soldiers filled the hospitals, Dix relaxed her standards; although she did continue to try to get women educated as nurses.

"Will you train nurses in your hospital for service in the U.S. Army?" she wrote to Elizabeth Blackwell, the first American woman to earn a medical degree and the founder of a hospital run by women and a medical school. "Not in my hospital, but at Bellevue Hospital, so the male surgeons may take credit!" Blackwell replied, well aware of the obstacles women faced.

Unlike many people at the beginning of the war, Dix wasn't fooled by talk of an easy victory and few casualties. While sightseers from Washington rode out with picnic baskets to watch the first major battle of the war around Manassas Junction near Bull Run Creek, Dorothea Dix stayed behind to prepare for casualties. When news of the disaster — 2,000 Union soldiers killed and wounded—reached her, she sent nurses to a makeshift hospital set up near the battlefield.

For days she mobilized nurses, distributed supplies, and inspected hospitals. The scene was horrendous as wounded soldiers staggered into the city after walking twenty-five miles from the battlefield—one with a large hole through both thighs, another with a hole through both cheeks, a broken jaw, and his tongue nearly torn off. A tangled assortment of amputated limbs was stacked up on the ground outside the hospitals, waiting to be carted off and buried. Garbage and human waste piled up in the streets. Epidemics of scurvy, dysentery, and typhoid swept the city.

Dorothea Dix and her nurses were everywhere, tending to the sick and wounded. In addition, Dorothea Dix kept a close eye on her nurses—taking over for a bit so they could rest, letting them live in her house until they had their own places, and sending them food (they were paid forty cents a day and one ration of food). Later on, when bills were introduced in Congress to give land grants to soldiers, Dorothea Dix always tried, unsuccessfully, to get her nurses included.

One of Dix's nurses was Louisa May Alcott, who became the world-famous author of *Little Women*. Alcott wrote in her diary about a time when she was very sick and, "Miss Dix brought a basket full of bottles of wine, tea, medicine, & cologne, beside a little blanket & pillow, a fan & a Testament. She is a kind soul but very queer & arbitrary." Alcott also wrote "no one likes her & I don't wonder," but then crossed the words out.

In particular Dix was disliked by the male doctors and officers, who resented her criticisms about how they ran the hospitals, along with her habit of always standing up for her nurses and patients whenever a problem arose. One much talked about incident happened at the convalescent hospital at Fortress Monroe in Hampton, Virginia. Dix discovered two convalescing patients strung up by their thumbs for disobeying a rule, by order of the medical officer in charge.

"Who is the superior here?" she asked General Butler, overall commander of the district, "the medical officer at Hampton or the Superintendent of Nurses for the Union Army?"

"By rank, the Superintendent of Nurses," Butler replied.

"Then I order those men cut down and the medical officer held on charges of inhumane conduct," Dix said. With that the men were cut down, the charges against them dropped, and the medical officer dismissed.

As the war continued, Dix's exacting manner made her more and more unpopular. Finally in October 1863, her authority was undermined by Order 351. Issued by Secretary of War Stanton, Order 351 allowed the surgeon-general to appoint nurses, which made Dix's approval no longer necessary. Dorothea Dix was crushed. Stanton, one of her most loyal admirers, had given in to pressure from disgruntled medical officers. Hurt and humiliated, Dorothea Dix considered resigning. But, no, she finally decided, there was too much work to do. She had to persevere.

Armed with passes of introduction from President Lincoln that said, "This introduces Miss Dix. Please receive her kindly and avail yourself of her services among the sick and wounded soldiers. A. Lincoln," Dorothea Dix traveled throughout the north, inspecting hospitals, checking up on her nurses, providing supplies, and visiting wounded soldiers.

"I saw a great deal of her during my hospital service," A.T. Perry, one of Dix's nurses, wrote years later. "A little old lady past sixty-five, but singularly youthful in her movements, looks, and especially in her voice, which was always so daintily modulated to fix its exact

The General Hospital at Fortress Monroe where Dorothea Dix frequently visited wounded soldiers. (Photo courtesy of Fort Monroe Casement Museum.)

weight upon her every word, and yet, as far as I knew her, so invariably potent in holding her listener at arm's length, it especially impressed me as her feature of very marked individuality. In dress she was the perfection of neatness ... She was perpetually on duty, and so thoroughly did she give herself, heart and soul, to her work, she seemed to know no weariness." Another nurse, Mary Olnhausen, remembered her as "A stern woman of few words."

Especially concerned about the soldiers' diet, Dorothea Dix harassed the Surgeon General to provide "a diet on which men can live, not die, before they even have a chance to fight for their country." When reports reached her that General Grant's army was dying faster from disease than from enemy bullets, she took matters into her own hands and sent out a special appeal that resulted in tons of fresh and canned vegetables and fruit being sent to the troops.

After three years of working nonstop, Dorothea Dix wrote, "Dear Annie—Time rolls on. We still measure its age by the flow and ebb of conflicts and battles ... When shall we have peace? is the cry of our hearts ..." A month later she wrote, "Our times are very sad, and events are hinging on so many uncertainties that I feel the best security from an overwhelming anxiety is in the careful performance of daily duty and daily reference to the precepts of our land."

A year later the war was over. Dorothea Dix stayed at her post, carrying out hundreds of requests that dying soldiers had given her, responding to requests from relatives looking for missing sons, husbands, fathers, and lovers, securing pensions for wounded soldiers, and visiting hospitals. Finally she resigned, one of the last people in command to leave the Union army. Few people served as long and as diligently as she did. Secretary of War Stanton insisted on honoring her.

What would she like, he asked her? Money from Congress? A day of recognition? Anything.

"The flag of my country," was all Dorothea Dix wanted.

Three years later, General Sherman presented a specially made stand of flags to Dorothea Dix by an act of Congress, the first woman to receive such an honor:

Order in Relation to the Services of Miss Dix:

In token and acknowledge of the inestimable services rendered by Miss Dorothea L. Dix for the care, succor, and relief of the sick and wounded soldiers of the United States on the battlefield, in camps, and hospitals during the recent war, and of her benevolent and diligent labors and devoted efforts to whatever might contribute to their comfort and welfare, it is ordered that a stand of arms of the United States colors be presented to Miss Dix."

Greatly honored, Dorothea Dix responded, "No greater distinction could have been conferred upon me … No possession will be so prized while life remains to love and serve my country."

While she had no regrets about serving her country, Dorothea Dix was greatly concerned about one thing—could she resume her crusade in the Southern states? Would she, who had served the Union Army and been so honored, be welcomed in those states, including North Carolina, Mississippi, Alabama, and Texas, that had lost the war?

Chapter Fourteen

NEVER QUIT

The war left 600,000 dead soldiers. Row after neat row of marble gravestones stretched across fields where horses and cows once grazed. One newly built cemetery in particular interested Dorothea Dix—the one where 6,000 soldiers were buried at Hampton, Virginia, near Fortress Monroe (today referred to as "old" Fort Monroe and the only fort of its type, completely surrounded by a water-filled moat, left in the United States). Not far from Washington, Fortress Monroe had a hospital that Dorothea had frequently visited to see wounded soldiers during the war. There she had received "... countless last messages of hundreds of dying men to fathers, mothers, wives, and children ..." When plans to build a monument at Fortress Monroe cemetery fell through because of lack of money, Dix took over. "Lately I have collected in a quiet way among my friends $8,000 with which to erect a granite monument in a cemetery at Fortress Monroe where are interred more than 6,000 of our brave, loyal soldiers ...," she wrote to Mrs. Rathbone. "I had special direction over most of these martyred to a sacred cause ... Thank heaven the war is over ..."

Going herself to a rock quarry in Maine, Dorothea

After the Civil War, Dorothea Dix raised money to build a Soldiers' Monument. With the laying of the cornerstone construction started on October 3, 1867. (Photo courtesy of Fort Monroe Casement Museum.)

Dorothea Dix selected the granite and designed the fence made out of muskets for the Soldiers' Monument, National Cemetery, Hampton, Virginia. (Photo courtesy of Fort Monroe Casement Museum.)

Photograph of Dorothea Lynde Dix taken when she was in her late sixties. (Reproduced by permission of the Houghton Library, Harvard University.)

selected a piece of granite to be shipped to Virginia. Cut into a sixty-five foot obelisk and placed on a massive base, the monument was surrounded by a circular fence (which Dix designed) made out of 1,000 muskets and bayonets, rifles, and twenty-four pound shot. In writing to congratulate her upon completion of the monument, her friend Dr. Isaac Ray wrote, "I congratulate you on the completion of your Monument. With so much stone and iron on your shoulders, I do not wonder you got sick. Pray, do take a lighter load the next time you shoulder other people's burdens."

Finally, in 1867 at the age of sixty-five, Dorothea Dix resumed her crusade. Despite the arduous life she had lived, her skin was smooth, her eyes bright, and her hair barely streaked with gray. Even now people still commented about her remarkable voice and stately bearing. Less than a hundred pounds, she moved as quickly as a woman half her age. For the next fifteen years, she traveled extensively.

She was honored and respected everywhere she went, including, much to her relief, in the South. "Dear Annie —" she wrote from Raleigh, North Carolina, "The citizens and public functionaries have met me with such unmistakable cordiality ..." In fact, she was invited to take a seat on the floor of the North Carolina senate as the "Honored Lady" and received a standing ovation from the senators. In the House of Representatives, she was introduced as "... Miss Dix, the eminent philanthropist ... Her name is a household word wherever civilization and Christian charity are known and respected."

The war had taken a terrible toll. "It would seem that all my work is to be done over so far as the insane are concerned. Language is too poor to describe the miserable state of these poor wretches in dungeon cells," she told her friend Mrs. Torrey. Undaunted, Dorothea Dix threw herself into her work. A third hospital was built in Pennsylvania (named Dixmont after her grandfather) "for which I have got an appropriation of $200,000," she wrote to a friend. Repairs were made to hospitals in South Carolina. Additions were built on hospitals in Tennessee, Ohio, and Kentucky.

Her crusade even spread to Japan through Arinori

Mori, a Japanese diplomat, whom Dix had influenced when he was stationed in Washington. "My Dear Miss Dix, —" Mori wrote several years after his return to Japan, "During the long silence, do not think I have been idle about the matter in which you take so deep an interest. I have given the subject much of my time and attention, and have successfully established an asylum for the insane at Kiyoto, and another in this city is being built and will soon be ready for its work of good. Other asylums will follow, too, and I ardently hope they will be the means of alleviating much misery."

In 1869, shortly after the first transcontinental railroad from New York to California was completed, Dorothea Dix left for California and Oregon. "Dear Annie —I cannot, of course, say how long I may be absent or how I shall return. Providence permitting the execution of my plans, I may be back before September."

Within months of her return from California, Dorothea collapsed. "Malaria in the most malignant form," her doctor said. "Her system has been saturated with it for years." For days she lingered between life and death. But before long, she rallied. "Dear Annie —," she wrote, "Gaining strength slowly but surely. Was partially dressed yesterday and wearing a lilac and white house dress which you gave me almost twenty years ago ..."

Obeying her doctor's orders to rest, Dorothea Dix slowed down a bit, but not much.

"Dear Annie —" she wrote during her recuperation, "Mail brings requests from ex-soldiers to look after their back pay and pensions, requests from seven person who have lost money registered and not transmitted by mail through various post offices ... a request to get three children, one an infant three months old, into the Foster Home; a request for a contribution to the Young Men's Christian Association; another for clothing for two families ...; opinions on the Woman's Rights and their fitness

123

for the learned professions, etc., and the best method for organizing and sustaining reform homes for fallen women, etc. . . .

"Now if you think I am idle any part of the working time for the twenty-four hours, you are mistaken. I have all the time and have always as much as I can do."

Before long Dorothea Dix was traveling again. Getting around the country was easier now (although during her trip to California she had had to spend twelve days on a horse and once rode twenty-five miles in one day). Trains were faster, cleaner, and safer. A network of paved roads connected towns and villages. Bridges had been built across rivers that Dix once splashed through in wagons. Considered a member of many families, Dorothea Dix looked forward to visiting them as she traveled around the country—the Eliots in Oregon, Kerlins in Pennsylvania, and Dobbins in North Carolina. She was particularly fond of her friends' children. "What can I send them," she asked their parents. "Will another five dollars get anything for Thanksgiving or Christmas, a small gift?"

Inevitably Dorothea Dix began to slow down. Increasingly her health failed. Mrs. S.C.P. Miller wrote an account of visiting Dix in a hotel in Richmond, Virginia. "I went to the hotel ... and there found such a Miss Dix as I had never dreamed of. Overstrain of mind and body, ... had left her stretched upon a sofa utterly weak, nervous, and tearful ... Amazed at her condition, I bent over her with a tenderness before unknown and a new bond of sympathy was established between us ..."

In October 1881 Dorothea Dix arrived at the New Jersey State Lunatic Asylum. She was very ill. So ill that Dr. John Ward, the superintendent and her admirer, told the board of directors of the hospital that

A post-Civil War portrait of Dorothea Dix. Her eyes reflect the pain and suffering she has seen, but also her determination to continue her work. (Reproduced by permission of the Houghton Library, Harvard University.)

Years after Dorothea Dix died, her apartment at the New Jersey State Lunatic Asylum (now called Trenton Psychiatric Hospital) was restored to look as it did when she lived there. (Photo courtesy of the Trenton Psychiatric Hospital, Trenton, New Jersey.)

125

she might not recover. Immediately the board authorized Dr. Ward "to make all necessary provision for the
convenience and comfort of Miss Dix while she remains in the Asylum."

Dorothea Dix remained in a small apartment set
aside for her in the hospital for five years. Frequently
in pain, she suffered as her hearing failed and her eyes
grew dim. But her mind remained sharp and her spirits positive. As she had throughout her life, she read
poems, hymns, and scriptures, over and over again.
John Greenleaf Whittier, the famous poet, sent her a
copy of his poem "At Last," which she kept under her
pillow.

In early 1882 she wrote to her friend Rose Lamb,
"I am still in invalid dress or rather undress, mostly on
the bed, with no prospect of being abroad when spring
flowers spring, bloom and blossom. There has been little wintry weather, the fields are more green than
brown. One heavy snowfall afforded two days sleighing
for patients. I gain strength slowly and have a vivid
sense of aloneness except when I read the cheering
blessed promises and example of our Lord." Her
beloved Annie had died four years earlier, as had her
brother Joseph. William Rathbone before that, Horace
Mann, Samuel Gridley Howe—so many were gone. Still
her life was full of other friends who wrote to her and
visited often. Superintendents sent her regular reports
and old students contacted her. "I never think of you as
grown old," wrote a former student from Cincinnati.
"You always come to me as I knew you first, crowned
with rich brown hair, the like of which no one else ever
had ..." Although Dorothea Dix was feeble and unable
to walk, her drive to live a life of purpose remained
strong, "I think even lying on my bed I can still do
something," she told Mrs. Miller in the spring of 1887.

Despite constant pain, Dorothea Dix resisted medication. "Don't give me anything," she instructed Dr. Ward. "None of those anodynes to dull senses or relieve pain. I want to—feel it all. And—please tell me when the time is near. I want to know."

The end came for Dorothea Dix on July 17, 1887.

"Just as I opened the door," Dr. Ward reported, "she heaved a soft, quiet sigh and all of earth was over."

According to her wishes, Dorothea Lynde Dix was buried at Mt. Auburn Cemetery in Cambridge, Massachusetts. It was a simple service attended by a few close friends. Some Scripture was recited, a few words were spoken, and "At Last" was read from the well-worn copy Dorothea Dix had kept under her pillow.

"When on my day of life the night is falling,
And, in the winds from unsunned spaces blown
I hear far voices out of darkness calling
My feet to paths unknown,
Those who hast made my home of life so pleasant,
Leave not its tenant when its walls decay;
O Love Divine, O Helper ever present,
Be Thou my strength and stay!"

A simple piece of marble marks Dorothea Dix's grave. There is no epitaph or date, only the words:

DOROTHEA L. DIX

Her life of purpose was over. But her example of the power of commitment, determination, astuteness, and a willingness to make sacrifices remains, as does her vision of humane treatment regardless of a person's condition or situation. "All alike may suffer," Dorothea Dix wrote, "the rich and the poor, the learned and the uneducated, the young, the mature, and the aged." Knowing that "all alike may suffer" didn't make Dorothea Lynde Dix give up hope. It didn't make her quit. Instead it inspired her to alleviate suffering, to overcome it, and to prove that one person can make a difference.

EPILOGUE

Undoubtedly Dorothea Dix would have a lot to say about the attitudes toward and the treatment of people with mental illness in America today. And she wouldn't be pleased. She would be horrified to see that some of her beloved state mental hospitals are closed down and others are merely serving as warehouses for people with a variety of conditions — mental retardation, chronic mental illness, alcoholism, drug addiction, the physical and mental deterioration of aging, and people without the money or skills to function anyplace else. She would be outraged at the plight of homeless people, many of whom suffer from mental illness. She would be indignant at the ignorance about mental illness and at the discrimination against people with mental illness—the names they're called, the jobs they can't get, and the places they aren't welcome. She would probably feel as she did after the Civil War, "It would seem that all my work is to be done over so far as the insane are concerned."

Even before Dorothea Dix died, her work needed to be done over again. During the 1880s, the state hospitals became severely overcrowded. Money was scarce. And Dorothea Dix, confined to her bed, could no longer carry on her crusade. In 1887, ironically just two months after Dix's death, a courageous newspaper reporter, Nellie Bly, investigated the conditions at the hospital for indigent mentally ill people on Blackwell's Island, a hospital Dix used to visit. Pretending to be mentally ill, Bly spent ten terrifying days in what she later described as a "human rat-trap." Finally her friends managed to get her released. "I left the insane ward with pleasure and regret," Bly wrote, "pleasure that I was once more able to enjoy the free breath of heaven; regret that I could not have brought with me some of the unfortunate women who lived and suffered with me."

The shocking newspaper exposé Bly wrote got national attention. Throughout America, the conditions at mental hospitals improved. But not for long. In 1934, John Maurice Grimes uncovered deplorable conditions in 600 state mental hospitals. In 1948 Albert Deutsch investigated hospitals and discovered that "In some of the wards there were scenes that rivaled the horrors of the Nazi concentration camps — hundreds of naked mental patients herded into huge, barnlike, filth-infested wards, in all degrees of deterioration, untended and untreated, stripped of every vestige of human decency, many in stages of semi-starvation." Again there were improvements. But, again, in 1955, a commission appointed by Congress concluded that state mental hospitals were "a 'dumping ground' ..." And so, the rollercoaster of reforms, exposés, reforms, exposés of mental hospital conditions continued.

Finally, in the late 1960s, state mental hospitals started to deinstitutionalize, or release, large numbers of patients. It was clear that Dorothea Dix's mental hospitals were no longer manageable. Now, the plan was for mentally ill people to live in smaller residences such as halfway houses or apartment buildings with counselors while they received treatment in community mental health centers. Unfortunately, many of the residences and community mental health centers never got built. And the ones that were built didn't have enough staff, facilities, or money to provide adequate care. Consequently, many deinstitutionalized mentally ill people were and still are left on their own.

As dismal as the current situation is for people with mental illness—especially if they are poor—there are some signs of hope. Modern researchers are discovering new ways to treat mental illness. An increasing number of people and organizations are working to improve community-based residences, programs, and treatment centers. Congress recently passed the Americans with Disabilities Act, which includes regulations to reduce discrimination against mentally ill people. And more information is being published to educate people about mental illness, including stories about famous people such as the writer William Styron, who recovered from a major depression, and the football star Lionel Aldridge, who overcame paranoid schizophrenia. Although Dorothea Lynde Dix's plan to build hospitals is no longer accepted, her vision of treating mentally ill people with dignity and respect and providing humane care is.

Readers who are interested in learning about mental illness and advocacy groups should contact:

The National Alliance for the Mentally Ill, 1901 North Ft. Myer Drive, Suite 500, Arlington, VA 22209;

The National Institute of Mental Health, Public Inquiries, Department P2, 5600 Fishers Lane, Room 15C05, Rockville, MD 20857;

National Mental Health Association, 1021 Prince Street, Alexandria, VA 22314.

CHRONOLOGY

April 4, 1802:   Dorothea (christened Dorothy) Lynde Dix born in Hampden, Maine.

1814:   Leaves home to live with grandmother in Boston.

1816:   Opens dame school in Worcester.

1819:   Returns to Boston, where she learns, learns, and learns everything she can.

1821:   Opens day and boarding school in Dix Mansion; also opens charitable school for poor children.

1824:   Publishes popular book for children, *Conversation on Common Things*.

1826:   Collapses from lung hemorrhages and exhaustion; closes schools.

1827-29:   Writes four more books, including a compendium of flowers.

1830:   Travels to St. Croix, Virgin Islands as tutor for children of William Ellery Channing.

1831:   Reopens day and boarding school and charitable school.

1836:	Collapses from lung hemorrhages and exhaustion; closes schools.
	Sails on *Baltic* for Liverpool, England.
1836-37:	Recuperates at Greenbank, the Rathbones' estate near Liverpool, England.
	Returns to Boston.
March 28, 1841:	Teaches Sunday School lesson to prisoners in East Cambridge jail; appalled at treatment of mentally ill people there.
1842:	Tours every place in Massachusetts where indigent mentally ill people are kept.
January 1843:	Presents Memorial to Massachusetts Legislature; starts investigation in Nova Scotia and New York.
1844:	Exposes mistreatment of mentally ill people in Rhode Island.
1845:	Presents Memorial to legislatures of New Jersey and Pennsylvania.
1845-46:	Conducts campaign in Tennessee, Kentucky, Ohio, and Maryland.
1846-47:	Launches crusade in the South — Louisiana, Alabama, Georgia, South Carolina, Mississippi, and Arkansas.
June 23, 1848:	Presents Memorial to Congress asking for 5,000,000 acres of public lands for care of indigent mentally ill people.

1849:	Takes campaign to Alabama, Mississippi, Louisiana, Illinois, Ohio, and North Carolina.
1850:	Land grant bill, now increased to 12,225,000, is passed by House of Representatives and deferred by Senate.
1851:	Land grant bill is passed by Senate and deferred by House.
1852:	Obtains Congressional approval for Army and Navy Hospital in Washington (today called St. Elizabeths).
1853:	Travels to Nova Scotia and Sable Island.
1854:	Land grant bill passes both House and Senate; vetoed by President Pierce in May.
Sept. 2, 1854:	*Sails on Arctic* for Liverpool, England.
February 1855:	Campaigns in Scotland and Channel Islands.
1856:	Tours Italy and intercedes with Pope Pius IX to improve treatment of mentally ill people in Rome; travels through Greece, Turkey, Austria-Hungary, Germany, Russia, and Scandinavian countries.
	Returns to America.
1857:	Resumes crusade for humane treatment of mentally ill people.

1858-9:	Travels to Texas and throughout the South.
1861:	Appointment as Superintendent of the Female Nurses of the Army.
1861-65:	Performs duties as Superintendent of Nurses.
1867:	Raises fund for Soldiers' Monument.
	Resumes crusade.
1869:	Travels to California.
1878:	Anne Heath dies.
1881:	Undertakes last tour of the South on October 1.
	Arrives in ill health at Trenton Hospital.
July 17, 1887:	Dies in apartment in Trenton, New Jersey.

FIRST ANNUAL REPORT OF THE SUPERINTENDENT OF THE NEW JERSEY STATE LUNATIC ASYLUM December 1848

Dorothea Dix was particularly fond of the New Jersey State Lunatic Asylum. It was the first brand new hospital built because of her efforts and the place where she spent the last five years of her life. The asylum opened on May 15, 1848. On December 31, H.A. Buttolph, M.D., the superintendent and physician, submitted the first annual report to the governor of New Jersey.

In his report, Buttolph described the asylum as "Reposing in the midst of the most beautiful scenery in the valley of the Delaware, combining all the influences which human art and skill can command to bless, soothe, and restore the wandering intellects that are gathered in its bosom, the state may profoundly point to this asylum, as a noble illustration of that charity, which, born from above, diffuses itself in blessings on the poor and unfortunate."

The following table was also included in the report. Of particular interest to modern readers are number 4 (occupations of the insane) and number 6 (alleged causes of insanity). The chart is as it appeared in the report.

The following tables exhibit, in a condensed form, the more important statistical records of the institution.

1....SEXES.	M.	W.	Tot.
	47	39	86
2....AGES.			
Between 10 and 15,	2	1	3
" 15 " 20,	2	5	7
" 20 " 30,	19	8	27
" 30 " 40,	6	11	17
" 40 " 50,	10	7	17
" 50 " 60,	4	5	9
" 60 " 70,	3	2	5
" 70 " 80,	1		1
	47	39	86
3....DOMESTIC STATE.			
Married,	17	13	30
Unmarried,	29	23	52
Widows,		3	3
Widowers,	1		1
	47	39	86
4....OCCUPATION.			
Farmers,	22		22
Seamstress,		1	1
Tailors,	2		2
Housekeepers,		16	16
Shipcarpenter,	1		1
Blacksmith,	1		1
Housework,		13	13
Writingmaster,	1		1
Milkman,	1		1
Clergyman,	1		1
Laborers,	3		3
Milliner,		1	1
Surveyor,	1		1
Mason,	1		1
Turner,	1		1
Factory work,	1	1	2
Mantuamakers,		2	2
Clerk,	1		1
Artificial flr. maker,		1	1
Merchant,	1		1
Cooper,	1		1
Student,	1		1
Nurse,		1	1
Shoemaker,	1		1
Miller,	1		1
Teachers,	1	1	2
Cabinetmaker,	1		1
No occupation,	3	2	5
	47	39	86

5....FORM OF DISEASE.	M.	W.	Tot.
Affections of intellect.			
Idiocy,	3		3
Imbecility,	12	9	21
Fatuity,		1	1
Mania with delusion,	6	2	8
" general,	9	10	19
Affections of sentiments.			
Melancholia,	4	6	10
Mon'a of fear,	1		1
" of pride,	1		1
" of suicide,	2	4	6
" of suspicion,	2	3	5
" of superstition,	3	2	5
Affections of propensities.			
Monomania, furious, or destructive,	4	2	6
	47	39	86
6....ALLEGED CAUSES.			
Ill health,	4	6	10
Loss of property,	3	1	4
Intemperance,	6	1	7
Death of friends,		2	2
Religious excitement,	4	4	8
Deafness and disease of brain,	1		1
Abuse of husband,		2	2
Domestic trouble,	3	3	6
Apoplexy,	1		1
Epilepsy,	1		1
Death of lover,		1	1
Injury of head,	2	1	3
Insanity of wife,	1		1
Congenital,	2		2
Stroke of sun,	1		1
Mormonism,	1		1
Meningitis,		1	1
Hard study,	2		2
Lawsuit,	1		1
Suppres'n of menses,		1	1
False accusation,		1	1
Fright,		1	1
Unknown,	14	14	28
	47	39	86

HISTORIC PLACES TO VISIT

Dorothea Dix's Grave, Mt. Auburn Cemetery, Cambridge, Massachusetts.

Directions to her grave are available at the cemetery headquarters located in the main parking lot.

Dorothea Dix Library and Museum, Harrisburg State Hospital, Harrisburg, Pennsylvania.

Open first Sunday and third Wednesday of every month 2-4 p.m. or by appointment.

Dorothea Dix Park, located at the southern end of Hampden, Maine along Route 1A.

Soldiers' Monument, Hampton National Cemetery, Hampton, Virginia. (The circular fence Dix designed is no longer there; it was removed after the wood rotted and the guns rusted.)

Dorothea Dix Portraits, National Portrait Gallery, Washington D.C. In addition, many hospitals have portraits of Dix such as St. Elizabeths Hospital, Washington, D.C.; Harrisburg State Hospital, Harrisburg, Pennsylvania; Butler Hospital, Providence, Rhode Island; Dorothea Dix Hospital, Raleigh, North Carolina; Central State Hospital, Nashville, Tennessee.

FURTHER READING

Elgin, Kathleen. *Angel of Mercy, Dorothea Lynde Dix.* Boston: David McKay Company, Inc., 1971.

Horwitz, Elinor L. *Madness, Magic, and Medicine: The Treatment and Mistreatment of the Mentally Ill.* New York: Harper & Row, 1977.

Marshall, Helen E. *Dorothea Dix, Forgotten Samaritan.* Chapel Hill, North Carolina: The University of North Carolina Press, 1937.

Synder, Charles M. *The Lady and the President, The Letters of Dorothea Dix and Millard Fillmore.* Lexington: University of Kentucky Press, 1975.

Tiffany, Francis. *Life of Dorothea Lynde Dix.* Boston: Houghton, Mifflin, 1891.

Wilson, Dorothy Clarke. *Stranger and Traveler.* Boston: Little, Brown and Company, 1975.

Zilboorg, Gregory. *A History of Medical Psychology.* New York: W.W. Norton, 1941.

INDEX